THE MUSE AND THE LIBRARIAN

CONTRIBUTIONS IN AMERICAN STUDIES

Series Editor: Robert H. Walker

1. The Rhetoric of American Politics: A Study of Documents
   William Raymond Smith

2. The Columbian Exchange: Biological and Cultural Consequences of 1492
   Alfred W. Crosby, Jr.

3. The Presidency of Rutherford B. Hayes
   Kenneth E. Davison

4. A Touchstone for Greatness: Essays, Addresses, and Occasional Pieces About Abraham Lincoln
   Roy P. Basler

5. The Politics of a Literary Man: William Gilmore Simms
   Jon L. Wakelyn

6. Visions of America: Eleven Literary Historical Essays
   Kenneth S. Lynn

7. The Collected Works of Abraham Lincoln. Supplement 1832-1865
   Roy P. Basler, Editor

8. Art and Politics: Cartoonists of the *Masses* and *Liberator*
   Richard Fitzgerald

9. Progress and Pragmatism: James, Dewey, Beard, and the American Idea of Progress
   David W. Marcell

THE MUSE AND THE LIBRARIAN

ROY P. BASLER

Contributions in American Studies, Number 10

Greenwood Press

Westport, Connecticut • London, England

Library of Congress Cataloging in Publication Data

Basler, Roy Prentice, 1906—
    The muse and the librarian.

    (Contributions in American studies, no. 10)
    CONTENTS: The muse and the librarian.—Yankee
Vergil—Robert Frost in Washington.—Your friend
the poet, [etc.]
    1. American poetry—20th century—Addresses,
essays, lectures. 2. Art patronage—United
States—Addresses, essays, lectures. I. Title.
PS324.B3   811'.5'09   72-780
ISBN 0-8371-6134-7

Library of Congress Catalog Card Number: 72-780
ISBN: 0-8371-6134-7
First published in 1974

Greenwood Press, a division of Williamhouse-Regency Inc.
51 Riverside Avenue, Westport, Connecticut 06880

Manufactured in the United States of America

CONTENTS

PREFACE

Of this collection of excursions in modern American literature, all but the first have appeared in various periodicals. They seem in retrospect, thus assembled, to deal with a common theme, struck inadvertently by the later discovery of Amy Lowell's lines apostrophizing the Library of Congress, and America — "this vast confused beauty," — ·as an appropriate beginning for the narrative entitled "The Muse and the Librarian."

Esthetic, as well as ethical and plain intellectual, confusion has seemed increasingly to characterize the almost incredible age in which the writer grew up, tried to become educated, and frequently failed to adequately understand what was going on in the world of arts and letters, no less than those other worlds of science and politics. This was particularly so during the third quarter of the century when his residence in the nation's capital gave an alleged, but dubious, over-all perspective.

The initial account, from which the book hopefully takes its not-inappropriate title, and the second narrative, attempt to relate a small chapter in the literary history of the United States. The other essays are merely divagations in the realm of life and letters. It is hoped that their recording of enthusiasms rather than verities, in the midst of confusion, may justify them to whatever audience they find.

ACKNOWLEDGMENTS

Portions of *The Muse and the Librarian* were previously published and copyrighted: "Yankee Vergil—Robert Frost in Washington" appeared in *Voyages, A National Literary Magazine*, Vol. II, No. 4, pp. 8-22, Spring 1969; "Your Friend the Poet, Carl Sandburg" appeared in *Midway*, Vol. 10, No. 2, pp. 3-15, Autumn 1969, copyright 1969 by the University of Chicago Press; "Proteus as Apollo: The Poetry of Merrill Moore" appeared in *The Literary Review*, Vol. I, No. 2, pp. 233-247, Winter 1957-1958, copyright 1958 by the Fairleigh Dickinson University Press; "The Poet as Composer—Lee Anderson" appeared in *The Sewanee Review*, Vol. LXXX, No. 1, pp. 157-167, Winter 1972, copyright 1972 by The University of the South; "A Letter to Ali Baba" appeared in *Prairie Schooner*, Vol. LXIII, No. 3, pp. 237-247, University of Nebraska Press, Fall 1969; "The Heart of Blackness: M. B. Tolson's Poetry" appeared in *New Letters*, Vol. 39, No. 3, pp. 63-76, University of Missouri-Kansas City, Spring 1973, copyright 1973 by the Curators of the University of Missouri; "A Literary Enthusiasm; or, The User Used" appeared in *Midway*, Vol. 11, No. 1, pp. 11-21, Summer 1970, copyright 1970 by the University of Chicago Press; "Who Do You Think You Are?" appeared in *Midway*, Vol. 8, No. 2, pp. 43-55, Autumn 1967, copyright 1967 by the University of Chicago Press; "The Taste of It: Observations on Current Erotic Poetry" appeared in *Mosaic, a Journal for the Comparative Study of Literature and Ideas*, Vol. VI, No. 3, pp. 93-105, Spring 1973, copyright 1973 by the University of Manitoba Press.

THE MUSE AND THE LIBRARIAN

THE MUSE AND THE LIBRARIAN

Seldom has an American poet been moved to write a poem about the Library of Congress, but when Amy Lowell did so in 1922 (*The Literary Digest International Book Review*, Vol. I, No. 1), she struck a prophetic note with her rhetorical question

> Where else in All America are we so symbolized?

and her equally rhetorical answer

> This is America
> This vast confused beauty. . .

She was obviously referring to the high renaissance architecture, but as the poem progresses to its poetic conclusion the reader wonders whether she intended a metaphor for something more interior as well.

> The implacable life of silent words,
> Of tumultuous stillness of never-ceasing music,
> Lost to being that so it may triumph
> And become the blood and heat and urge

3

> Of that hidden distance which forever whips
>   and harries the present
> Of mankind.*

Her letter of December 2, 1922, protesting to the editor that the typesetters had garbled her lines "to the utter confusion of the poem," appeared with what was presumably the ungarbled poem in the *Review*'s second number. The last six lines just quoted remained unchanged, however, to leave no doubt in the reader's mind as to the Library's affair with the muse — a matter of the heart, as much as of the mind.

It would seem that Librarian of Congress Herbert Putnam had something less passionate in view for establishing various endowed "chairs" and consultantships, including the "chair of poetry" to be occupied by a "consultant in poetry." He set forth his views in the very first issue of *The Library Quarterly*, June 1931 (pp. 18-19): "The affiliation with the staff of a library of a group of such specialists representing at least the main fields of learning might bring to its service their criticism and suggestion in the development of the collections (and even the perfection of the apparatus), and might bring to the reader the benefit of their counsel in his actual use of the material and apparatus."

The requisite endowment to support the chair of "a Consultant in Poetry (in the English language)" was not forthcoming for six years. It was announced in the Librarian's *Annual Report* for 1937 (p. 4) that a benefactor "preferring, as always, to be anonymous" (Archer M. Huntington, who also liberally endowed the cause of Hispanic literature in the Library of Congress) had made the necessary contribution, and in addition: "It has been promptly taken advantage of by the engagement for the present year of Mr. Joseph Auslander, well known in the field of poetry, lecturer in poetry at Columbia University during the past 8 years and poetry editor of the *North American Review*." (*Ibid.*) Mr. Auslander's appointment was annually

---

* "The Congressional Library," *The Complete Poetical Works of Amy Lowell.* Houghton Mifflin Company, pp. 452-453.
Quoted by permission of the publisher.

renewed for the next five years and his title expanded to "Consultant in Poetry and Drama."

The Consultant's annual reports began in 1938 and indicated a variety of duties and accomplishments, perhaps most notably a nationwide itinerary of speaking engagements before poetry societies, groups of English teachers, and college audiences. Closer to home, he pursued the acquisition for the "Poetry Archives" of significant literary manuscript gifts from numerous authors and one particularly generous donor. The *Annual Report* for 1937, following announcement of Auslander's appointment, recorded that "In another cultural field — that of Music — our permanent resources have recently (in September 1937) been enhanced by the addition by Mrs. Gertrude Whittall of $50,000 to her endowment of $100,000 made 2 years ago." (p. 5) It might reasonably be inferred, even were not the oral tradition rampant, that the Consultant in Poetry had not been an idle acolyte of the muse, for it was reported in 1938 that Mrs. Whittall had given to the Library's Poetry Archives the holograph of E. A. Robinson's *Lancelot,* and again, in 1939, the Watts-Dunton collection of Rossetti manuscripts. Whatever opinion might obtain of the Poetry Consultant's accomplishments as a poet, romantic and sentimental as he was, his sonnets indited to Mrs. Whittall, as tradition saith, were not amiss, and her gifts of poetry manuscripts continued for many years to enrich the Library's manuscript collections with important items, such as the A. E. Housman notebooks and numerous E. A. Robinson holographs.

Auslander's notable success in this regard became the occasion, or the excuse, for his unseating, since the Librarian's *Annual Report* for 1942 lists him as "Gift Officer." The chair of poetry was temporarily vacant, but let it not be supposed that the muse went unwooed in "the vast, confused beauty" of those marble halls, for with the ascension of Herbert Putnam to the status "Librarian Emeritus," the poet-statesman Archibald MacLeish had been appointed by President Franklin D. Roosevelt to the office of Librarian of Congress beginning October 1, 1939. As Librarian of Congress, MacLeish performed a number of operations—amputations, ectomies, transplants, and mere

grafts — on the organizational body of the Library, some of
which were viable and would achieve far-reaching effects and
some of which simply did not "take." The position of "Gift Officer" disappeared, and with it Mr. Auslander, from the pages of
the Librarian's *Annual Report*, but the position of Consultant in
Poetry reappeared in 1943 with an incumbent, the ex- "Fugitive" Allen Tate.

Equally notable with MacLeish's reorganizations of the
Library's procedures and management was his new emphasis on
literary events and recognitions, to which he devoted his per-
sonal attention. His appointments of the French diplomat-poet
Alexis Saint-Leger (St.-John Perse) as Consultant in French
Literature and of Thomas Mann as Consultant in Germanic
Literature, for example, brought a level of literary distinction
not hitherto carried by even the most noteworthy of the
Library's roster of "specialists." The Library's Coolidge
Auditorium was no longer famous merely for the excellence of
its musical performances, but afforded standing-room-only, and
turned away many, for the series of poetry readings by Carl
Sandburg, Robert Frost, Robinson Jeffers, and Stephen Vincent
Benét, inaugurated in 1941 by means of a gift from Mr. and Mrs.
Eugene Meyer. Among other literary events, the presentation of
Sidney Kingsley's play *The Patriots* marked the Library's
observance of the Jefferson Bicentennial in 1943. Lectures by
Thomas Mann were a regular chore in his Consultantship in
Germanic Literature, beginning in 1942. The Consultant in
Poetry, however, seems neither to have read poems nor lectured
in the Coolidge Auditorium in an official capacity during the
MacLeish era. This practice began later, with the initial reading
by Poetry Consultant Leonie Adams in 1949, but it developed as
a regular duty only with the appointment of Randall Jarrell in
1956.

The duties conceived for the Consultantship in Poetry have
varied over more than a quarter century and with a succession
of twenty-one incumbents. In announcing the original appointment of Joseph Auslander, Librarian Putnam made it clear that
"As in the case of other consultants, the service to us will not
preclude those other interests, nor in his case necessitate contin-

uous residence in Washington." As with other consultantships, "development of the collections" and "perfecting its collections" were the phrases most emphasized in the original Putnam concept. With the appointment of Allen Tate, this emphasis continued and new editorial responsibilities were added.

Librarian MacLeish had warned Archer M. Huntington, the donor of the Fund which provided the salary of the Consultant in Poetry, of his conception of the possible use of the "Chair" in a letter dated September 13, 1940. It was MacLeish's feeling "that the Chair of Poetry . . . . could be made a source of great strength to American poetry by making it available to a succession of poets who would use it not as a Library position for Library purposes, but as a means of carrying on their own work for a period. Over the course of many years, the Library would be enriched by the presence from time to time of such men. The occupants of the Chair would be enriched by the experiences of the Library and the world which immediately surrounds and the award would become, I should suppose, one of the greatest distinctions in American letters."* And on April 19, 1943, MacLeish reported to Huntington that "it has finally been possible to arrange for the use of the Chair of Poetry in the manner you and I talked in New York some time ago. As you will recall, it has been my feeling that the importance of the Chair of Poetry . . . is so great that it should be filled from year to year by distinguished men of letters who will bring to the Library a contact . . . ." etc. To which Huntington replied on May 1, 1943: "This is real news! I rejoice with you in the permanent warming of the Poetry Chair. It will help to stave off the hour when the poets will be found in the coolers of the black market, with muskrats and horses!"

Huntington's humorous metaphor may seem something more than a bitter reminder of the temper of the times, black markets and concentration camps, perhaps even suggestive, in its possibilities for misinterpretation, of the metaphor of horror that was characterizing the poetry being written by an expatriate American poet who had espoused the Hitler-Mussolini Axis and

---

* This letter and others cited in the following pages are in the files of the Library of Congress, unless another source is cited.

would ere long come to play a role in the Library's poetic drama. None of this, however, could have been guessed by Librarian MacLeish when he recounted in his *Annual Report* for 1944 (pp. 35-36) the achievements of the new Consultant in Poetry, along with the prospects for his successor.

> The Library's Consultant in Poetry in English during the past year was Allen Tate, eminent American poet and critic. Mr. Tate entered upon his work with enthusiasm and undertook immediately a survey of our collection in American and English poetry. He had the valuable assistance of Frances Cheney, previously the Reference Librarian at Vanderbilt University, and, as a result, he was able to compile a number of want-lists which have already been used for the strengthening of our collections in the fields of his particular interest. In addition to his general activities in the field of American literature, Mr. Tate was given the specific responsibility of launching *The Quarterly Journal of Current Acquisitions.* The task of preparing copy from the raw material coming into the Library and from the pens of officers of the Library burdened by administrative responsibilities was a difficult one, but Mr. Tate met it with a success which was possible only to an accomplished editor. The first four issues of the *Journal* are a tribute to Mr. Tate's intelligent devotion. At the completion of his year Mr. Tate left the Library to edit *The Sewanee Review.*
>
> Robert Penn Warren, who has earned distinction as a man of letters in verse, biography, and the novel, has succeeded Mr. Tate as Consultant in Poetry in English. He has assumed also editorial responsibility for the *Quarterly Journal of Current Acquisitions.* Mr. Warren is a member of the faculty of the University of Minnesota, from which institution he comes to the Library on leave of absence.

More portentous, but for a quite different reason than the Librarian prophesied, was the further announcement (p. 38):

> Mr. Tate proposed and was largely instrumental in establishing a group of Fellows whose activities may eventually have a profound effect upon the collections of the Library — the Fellows of the Library of Congress in American Letters. The members of

this group, which met for the first time on May 26-27, are: Katherine Garrison Chapin (Mrs. Francis Biddle), Katherine Anne Porter, Willard Thorp, Mark Van Doren, Van Wyck Brooks, Paul Green, Allen Tate, and Carl Sandburg.

For the reader's convenience it may be well at this point to list the first nine Consultants in Poetry and their respective terms of office:

Joseph Auslander	1937-1941
Allen Tate	1943-1944
Robert Penn Warren	1944-1945
Louise Bogan	1945-1946
Karl Shapiro	1946-1947
Robert Lowell	1947-1948
Leonie Adams	1948-1949
Elizabeth Bishop	1949-1950
Conrad Aiken	1950-1952

A notable further development during the decade that began with the appointment of Allen Tate was the inauguration by Robert Penn Warren, at Tate's suggestion, of a program to record poets, and occasionally novelists, reading selections from their own works. This activity has continued for more than a quarter century and has made the Library's Archive of Recorded Poetry and Literature one of the preeminent repositories of literary sound recordings. Logically enough, a corollary project was conceived to develop a series of recordings for sale to the public, entitled "Twentieth Century Poetry in English." This pioneering venture would prove to occupy a large portion of the time of each of the Consultants in selecting poets and poems for many years, with the resulting issuance by the Library's Recording Laboratory in 1949 of the "First Series," comprised of readings by 21 poets, and in 1952 of the "Second Series" comprised of readings by a "younger" group of 21 poets. Both series were made possible by grants from the Bollingen Foundation. New recordings of additional poets have continued to be issued by the Library from time to time, under other grants, notably by

the Ambrook Foundation, and the impact of the Library's
pioneering may be seen in the extensive lists of literary recordings included in the catalogs issued by commercial recording
companies in more recent years. Poetry has become a staple, if
limited, commodity of the record industry.

This happy collaboration between the Library of Congress and
the Bollingen Foundation in making modern poetry available
through modern technology suggested still another possibility —
the awarding of a quasi-national prize for the best book of
poetry published each year. Creation of the Bollingen Prize in
Poetry was announced by MacLeish's successor as Librarian of
Congress, Luther H. Evans, in a Press Release (No. 467) dated
March 4, 1948.

> The amount of the prize is one thousand dollars, and the jury
> may decline to make an award for any year if in its judgment no
> poetry worthy of the prize was published during that year. The
> award for 1948 will be announced by the Librarian of Congress in
> February 1949.
>
> The Jury of Selection will be composed of the Fellows in
> American Letters of the Library of Congress who at the present
> time are W.H. Auden, Conrad Aiken, Louise Bogan, Katherine
> Garrison Chapin, T.S. Eliot, Paul Green, Robert Lowell, Willard
> Thorp, Katherine Anne Porter, Karl Shapiro, Theodore Spencer,
> Allen Tate and Robert Penn Warren.
>
> The Bollingen Prize will be awarded to the author of the book of
> verse which in the opinion of the Fellows in American Letters
> represents the highest achievement of American poetry in the
> preceding year. Poets who are citizens of the United States either
> by birth or naturalization, or who were born in the United States
> but have become citizens of other countries, are eligible for the
> prize. No member of the group of Fellows in American Letters
> shall be eligible unless he shall have ceased to be a member for a
> period of two years before he publishes a book that may be con-
> sidered by the Jury.

Following the resignation of Archibald MacLeish on
December 19, 1944, to become Assistant Secretary of State,
Chief Assistant Librarian Luther Evans acted as Librarian until
his appointment by President Truman was confirmed by the

Senate, June 29, 1945. Thus, most of the literary activities which had been set in motion during the brief but fecund MacLeish regime were continued, expanded, and brought to fruition under Evans' administration — among them, those of the Fellows in American Letters. The membership of the Fellows had increased in number and shifted somewhat in literary complexion since MacLeish had appointed the first group in 1944. This might have seemed obvious to the observant literary eye scanning Evans' press release, but its implications were widely overlooked or ignored until February 20, 1949, when the Library announced to the press that the prize had been awarded to *The Pisan Cantos* of Ezra Pound, with the verdict of the Fellows justified in their words as follows:

> The Fellows are aware that objections may be made to awarding a prize to a man situated as is Mr. Pound. In their view, however, the possibility of such objection did not alter the responsibility assumed by the Jury of Selection. This was to make a choice for the award among the eligible books, provided any one merited such recognition, according to the stated terms of the Bollingen Prize. To permit other considerations than that of poetic achievement to sway the decision would destroy the significance of the award and would in principle deny the validity of that objective perception of value on which any civilized society must rest. (Press Release No. 542)

This statement of principle vastly oversimplified the case. Much soul-searching went on in the meetings and the correspondence among the Fellows prior to the announcement of the award. Their verdict had not been unanimous, nor had all among the majority been equally convinced either of the necessity or the desirability of awarding the prize to Pound. At the center was Robert Lowell, with Allen Tate his buttress, in spite of major personal objections to some of the *Pisan Cantos'* content and recognition that the overall poetic quality of the *Cantos* was uneven. Of course, the papal dignity of T. S. Eliot, who had dubbed Pound "il miglior fabbro," in dedicating *The Waste Land*, cannot be overestimated, but the nub of consensus among those who voted for Pound seems to have been simply that Pound's book

was far and away the outstanding book of poetry published in
1948, and that since this was so there was no alternative.
Pound's book was too good for the Fellows to maintain that
there was no book of sufficient poetic merit to warrant the prize,
and thus to recommend that no award should be made. They
were not unaware, however, that the function of the Library of
Congress as dispenser of a quasi-national prize would probably
be destroyed and that their function as Fellows in the Library
would therefore be circumscribed, if not completely impaired.
But there is no evidence that up to this point any book other
than Pound's was ever a serious contender for the Fellows' verdict, or that there was any serious concerted objection to the
poem's content, anti-American, anti-Semitic, anti-democratic,
and pro-Axis though it admittedly was in some parts. It was
judged as a brilliant, sometimes confused, poetic eruption that
expressed a poet's passionate and unrational rationale in a world
and a civilization he particularly hated, and loved. A quarter
century had elapsed since Amy Lowell apostrophized "the implacable life of silent words"!

Fellow Karl Shapiro, who had voted against the award, was to
point out some weeks later in *Partisan Review* (May 1949, p.
519) that the Fellows were made up largely "of those who had
come under his [Pound's] influence as impressario and teacher,
those who had at some time made declarations of political reaction, and those who had engaged in the literary struggle to dissociate art from social injunction. The presence of Mr. Eliot at
the meeting gave these facts a reality which perhaps inhibited
open discussion." As one particularly close observer of the
Fellows' deliberations put it privately at the time, they were all
"standing under the mistletoe."

Still later, in *Poetry and Opinion* (1950), Archibald MacLeish
was to attempt a defense by way of explanation, that Pound's
loyalty "is not to dogmas of fascism but to the poet's vision of a
tragic disorder which lies much deeper in our lives and in our
time" (p. 48) — an idea that may have occurred to, but seems not
to have been expressed by, the Fellows at the time. Perhaps the
best explanation of the verdict of the Fellows, however, was
poetic-critic John Berryman's paraphrase of Renoir's alleged

phrase, "I paint with my penis": ". . . we poets write verse with our ears . . . . that ear is one of the main, weird facts of modern verse. It imposes on the piteous stuff of the *Pisan Cantos* a 'distance' . . . The poet has listened to his life, so to speak, and he tells us that which he hears." ("The Poetry of Ezra Pound," *Partisan Review*, April 1949, p. 389).

This traditional esthetic escape hatch, in which the ancient poet's inspiration of the muse transmogrifies into "listening to his life," was hardly a satisfactory justification for an accolade from anyone not a poet, and certainly not from one whose ear was something less than sophisticated, as Librarian Evans would shortly avow.

The immediate reception in the press of the Fellows' announcement on February 20 was scarcely indicative of the storm to come. An article by Tom O'Hara in the New York *Herald Tribune* on the following day speculated on the mystery of the name "Bollingen" and quoted "poet and poetry anthologist" Louis Untermeyer and Robert Hillyer, "another prominent writer of poetry," as in general disagreement with the award. Hillyer's dissenting remarks as quoted emphasized that "the prize followed 'the fashion of modern critics and poets' . . . advanced by 'pressure groups' whose tactics are 'thorough and penetrating,' " a foreboding hint at most. But an editorial in the same issue, noting the Fellows' announcement of their awareness "that objections may be made," as seeming "somewhat on the defensive," went on to wonder whether "these objections will in reality be either vociferous or widespread." The editorial generally commended the Fellows for reaffirming "the principle that the value of art is independent of the moral character of the individual who produces it, as it may be independent of the subject matter with which it deals." Mild though these reactions seemed, they drew the lines for the literary battle that ensued in *The Saturday Review of Literature*, as well as in other literary journals and the press, and that spilled over into the pages of the *Congressional Record*.

Hillyer's coolly savage article bearing the title "Treason's Strange Fruit—The Case of Ezra Pound and the Bollingen Award," appeared in the *Review* on June 11, 1949, along with an

editorial by Harrison Smith and Norman Cousins attacking the
award, the Fellows, and the Library of Congress. The implications of the award and of the poetry to which the award was
made were Hillyer's primary concern. He affected to perceive
implications of a sinister infiltration of fascism into the Library
of Congress, via the Bollingen Foundation, via the teaching of
Carl Jung, who allegedly espoused Hitlerism. He also suspected
the infiltration was engineered by a majority of the Fellows as
disciples of Eliot and Pound, who not only shared the former's
estheticism but also the latter's fascism, and the anti-Semitism
of both these masters, in order to undermine American democracy and literary culture. Hillyer particularly inveighed against
the literary "priesthood" whose "gods" were Eliot and Pound,
and whose "power is enormous," he wrote, "especially in the colleges and even the preparatory schools," and has been used to
"subtly undermine reputations of our great poets such as Robinson and Frost."

The Fellows ably defended themselves against Hillyer's
allegations in a collectively signed protest and in several individual statements. Playwright Paul Green, the one Fellow who did
not sign the protest, received a query from editor Harrison
Smith and telegraphed good humoredly on July 12:

> I am not indignant about anything. I think the laugh is on us
> Fellows of the Library of Congress in American Letters for giving
> the Bollingen Award to Ezra Pound's book. I am willing to let it
> go at that. Naturally everybody agrees with the fine statement of
> Dr. Evans that literary judgments and preferences like other
> matters of the mind should be free. They certainly were in this
> matter. (Quoted by letter of Leonie Adams to Karl Shapiro, July
> 14, 1949)

Librarian Evans, never at a loss for words, responded in a
lengthy letter addressed to editor Norman Cousins on June 14.
Among many telling paragraphs, one stood out as the heart of
the Library's case.

> I personally regard the choice of *Pisan Cantos* for the Bollingen
> prize as an unfortunate choice. I do not feel called upon to go into

all of my reasons for feeling this. I think it is sufficient to say that from my poetically ignorant point of view, Mr. Pound's book is hardly poetry at all. I believe now, as I believed at the time of announcing the award, that I would be engaging in an improper interference with free scholarship if I were to substitute my own decision in this matter for the decision of the Fellows. I think that for me to interfere with the work of scholars would be far worse than to award the prize for a book which did not deserve it. After all, a cure is available in scholarly terms for scholarly errors, but I know of no cure for the bureaucratic error of overriding scholarly judgment in cases of this kind. I feel that I would have been striking a blow against the cause of liberty by overriding scholarly judgment, and I do not feel that the blow for unrighteousness which the award may represent, is nearly as grave. (*Congressional Record Appendix,* 1949, p. A4829)

Scarcely anyone took issue with Evans, and T.S. Eliot among others dubbed the statement "admirable." Editors Smith and Cousins, however, were not to be put off. There was still an issue unresolved to their satisfaction.

Mr. Evans says that he personally regards the choice of the *Pisan Cantos* as unfortunate, and offers his own view that it was hardly poetry at all. He believes, however, that it was hardly his function as Librarian of Congress to impose his own views on the Fellows of the Library of Congress who made the selection. We agree. We did not suggest that Mr. Evans should have substituted his own judgment for that of the Fellows. Once the Fellows made their selection, the fat was in the fire. We insist, however, that once the name of the Library of Congress was attached to the award it could not avoid responsibility. If the award was to have been an independent one, having nothing to do with a Government agency, then care should have been taken to dissociate the agency both from the committee making the award and from the award itself. But the United States Library of Congress cannot sponsor such an award as an integral part of its activities and then abruptly disclaim responsibility at the first sign of a fight. (*Ibid.*)

That issue was resolved on August 19, 1949, when the Joint Committee of the Congress on the Library unanimously voted that the Library should abstain from the giving of prizes or the making of awards. Not only the Bollingen Prize, but also the Elizabeth Sprague Coolidge Medal "for eminent services to chamber music," as well as three Library awards connected with the annual national exhibition of prints, were thus jettisoned. The Bollingen Prize, however, was to continue under the aegis of Yale University.

Among the embattled, Librarian Evans seems to have come off personally best of all. The Fellows unanimously commended him on January 20, 1950, by a Resolution on his "directness and courage, and his upholding of their freedom of judgment." (Minutes) But the Library of Congress, and perhaps the citizens of the United States to whose service it is ultimately dedicated, came off worst of all. For the Library's defeat in the effort to recognize high achievement in the arts on an official national (governmental) level would remain a sad, if not quite a tragic, episode in our cultural history. During the entire embroglio, Consultant in Poetry Leonie Adams performed not only the usual duties of her office, but also frequently more onerous tasks of drafter of drafts, spokesman, and liaison for the Fellows and the Librarian of Congress.

One cannot peruse the records of this affair without a sense that everyone was enjoying the bloodless fight tremendously, especially the Fellows. Likewise, one has the sense that no one was finally convinced of any but his own right or wrong, but that each was fully cognizant of his righteousness, whether it was esthetic, political, or moral righteousness he defended with such vigor of words.

Perhaps the separation of church and state, seen as the *sine qua non* of democracy by the founding fathers, carries a corollary: let everyman be his own judge of poetry! Arbiters of poetic taste we will always have with us, but let them never achieve even quasi-official status!

In retrospect, perhaps the irony of ironies in this episode may ultimately seem to be that few, if any, understood, and none stepped forward to elucidate, that Pound's *Pisan Cantos* were integral components of the only poem worthy of the term "epic" produced in our age, on what litterateurs and chamber of commerce evangelists alike have chosen to refer to as "the American Dream," frequently without knowing the difference between dream and reality. For certainly Pound's *Cantos*, whatever the faults, more than any other modern American poem, is thoroughly imbued with "the spirit of '76," preoccupied with revolution (i.e., "the revolt of intelligence" as Pound saw it), and infused with the informing myth of a possible new world, yet evolving under the impulse and impact of what Lincoln once called "the last best hope of earth." Unlike most modern poets, Pound really believed in "The enormous tragedy of the dream in the peasant's bent shoulders," that first line of the controversial *Pisan Cantos* which almost by itself justifies the award after so many years of continuing failure and betrayal in the satrapies of science and technology no less than in the seats of the mighty, politics and economics personified.

Perhaps a minor irony is suggested in a letter which Pound had written a decade earlier to newly appointed Librarian of Congress Archibald MacLeish, on July 19, 1939. Pound began, "Hearty if delayed congrats/on being raised to the head of a new profession." Alluding to the clamor on the part of professional librarians protesting MacLeish's appointment, he continued, "I think you cd/sqush hostile criticism by a couple of star plays, or if above such mere strife I shd/be glad if you wd/git on wiff 'em ANYhow. I had already opened the subjects while in Washington, both with Mr. Putnam and the Hist. and Music depts."

What Pound went on to lay before MacLeish was his proposal that the Library of Congress "get the Italian point of view re/barter" in order to obtain "priceless historic documents" in return for "one of those new machines for taking etc/& printing in 7 minutes which Dr. Spivack ect. [*sic*] showed me." And he needled with a compliment to MacLeish's predecessor, "Hang it, Putnam did such a MAGnificent job that anyone who succeeds him has got to show a leg."

As a semi-official consultant and advisor, Pound had previously laid his proposal before Librarian Herbert Putnam at a Round Table Luncheon, but it would be many years before the copying program already undertaken by the Library of Congress, with the war and its dislodgements intervening, would bear notable fruits. A world had turned sour indeed, in the decade between 1939 and 1949, but it would turn even sourer. When in 1958 Pound was released from custody in St. Elizabeth's Hospital, Herman A. Sieber, the young research analyst in the Library's Legislative Reference Service who had prepared "The Medical, Legal, Literary, and Political Status of Ezra Weston (Loomis) Pound, Selected Facts and Comments," which Representative Usher L. Burdick had inserted in the *Congressional Record*,* ascertained that Pound retained the friendliest of feelings toward the Library of Congress and would indeed be willing to visit its Recording Laboratory to read from his *Cantos.* The epidemic of McCarthyitis which had ravaged all government agencies was ebbing but by no means past, and the Library administration declined to permit an invitation to be extended to Pound. Thus, there is to this day not a single recording of Pound in the Library's extensive Archive of Recorded Poetry.

Although Librarian Evans addressed the next convocation of the Fellows on January 20, 1950, in hopeful terms, and suggested that they go on as they had been accustomed to do, things would never again be the same. What had originally been conceived as the more important functions of the Fellows, to advise in acquisitions, the preparation of bibliographies, and in any matters involving the furtherance of the Library's programs (*Annual Report*, 1944, p. 35 ff.), had not greatly interested them in recent meetings or prompted much activity. Their principal function thereafter would be to give advice on the appointment of additional fellows to their collegium and to the post of Consultant in Poetry. It was with the Consultant, after all, that the Library's affair with poetry began, and continued with dignity, distinction, and solid accomplishment until the appointment of Dr. William Carlos Williams brewed a second literary storm of somewhat lesser proportions. A factual chronology of

* April 29, 30, May 6, May 15, 1958: pp. A3894-3901, A3941-3945, A4157-58, A4172-4174, A4527.

this long-drawn and much misunderstood episode may be summarized.

In February 1948, Dr. Williams was first offered appointment as Consultant in Poetry for the 1949-1950 term, to follow Leonie Adams. He accepted in March and both his and Miss Adams' appointments were announced on March 16. On October 28, he wrote that because of illness it would not be wise for him to accept the responsibility. When the Librarian offered him appointment as one of the Fellows in American Letters, however, he was pleased to accept.

In April 1951 Dr. Williams suffered a heart attack, but in March 1952 he indicated to Consultant in Poetry Conrad Aiken that he once more was interested and was now able to accept the appointment, and Verner W. Clapp, Acting Librarian of Congress in Dr. Evans' absence, wrote on March 21 offering Williams the post beginning in September 1952. Williams accepted, and on August 8 the Library issued a press release announcing his appointment a second time, effective September 17, 1952. Once again illness intervened, and, at the request of his wife, Williams was granted a delay of three months before he would report for duty.

As required by the President's Executive Order 9835, March 21, 1947, appointments to positions in the federal government were (and are!) subject to loyalty investigations. Even honorary or *quasi* positions, with or without compensation, were then subject to this process, and as was customary, the Civil Service Commission was requested to compile a preliminary report on Dr. Williams. On December 4, just prior to the pending arrival of Dr. and Mrs. Williams, Chief Assistant Librarian Clapp wrote to Mrs. Williams that the Librarian would be out of town when they arrived and that he would see them instead; that he regretted to tell her a preliminary report resulting from the loyalty investigation made it necessary to ask for a full investigation; that Dr. Williams could not enter on his duties pending results of the full investigation; and that he was sending this message to Dr. Williams through her out of regard for Dr. Williams' health.

Dr. and Mrs. Williams met with the Acting Librarian and other members of the Library staff on their arrival; the loyalty processes, which had become increasingly exacerbating with the onset of the "McCarthy Era," were explained to them, and they were told that a hearing before the Library's Loyalty Board would be afforded if necessary after the full report had been received and evaluated. The visit terminated on a friendly note, but Dr. Williams, obviously still in delicate health, seemed to be understandably annoyed and non-plussed.

On December 22, 1952, James F. Murray, Jr., attorney at law, New York City, wrote three letters to the Chief Assistant Librarian and others at the Library advising them that Dr. Williams had retained him as his attorney and asserting Dr. Williams' right to assume the position and rights to salary thereunder.

On January 13, 1953, Librarian Evans wrote to Dr. Williams that he had determined that the conditions which had once seemed to make the appointment desirable and profitable no longer existed; that the change in conditions resulted not only from the Library's view of Dr. Williams' present state of health but also from new elements introduced into the relationship between Dr. Williams and the Library by Attorney Murray's letters; that he accordingly revoked the offer of appointment and terminated the negotiations which had been in progress in looking towards Dr. Williams' assumption of duties. The Librarian stated that he wished to make it very clear that this action had nothing to do with any allegations regarding Dr. Williams' loyalty which may have been published in various places, nor with the routine loyalty investigation initiated under the Federal Employees Loyalty Program, which would now be cancelled.

In February 1953, on behalf of several Fellows in American Letters who felt there was misunderstanding on both sides, former Consultant in Poetry Leonie Adams requested that they be permitted to serve as intermediaries on behalf of Dr. Williams. The Librarian met with her and Professor Cleanth Brooks on February 8, 1953, and on February 16 wrote Miss Adams to the effect that, assuming Dr. Williams was ready to disavow the assertions of a claim to rights connected with the Library's disallowance of his assumption of duties, he (Dr. Evans) was ready to consider sympathetically a statement from a qualified physician that Dr. Williams would probably be able to discharge the duties of the post, as of a given date and on a full-time or half-time basis, extending for a substantial period not exceeding the end of the period of the original appointment, i.e., September 1953. Should an offer of appointment result, Dr. Evans stated in his letter, and should Dr. Williams accept, Dr. Evans would notify the Civil Service Commission of the fact and request an expeditious completion of the full-field investigation which had been suspended, so that the preliminaries to an assumption of duties might be concluded in time to avoid any additional delay. He added that the loyalty clearance must precede the beginning of employment.

When all these conditions had been met, on April 24, 1953, Dr. Evans wrote Attorney Murray that he was appointing Dr. Williams as Consultant in Poetry in English, effective May 15, 1953, or as soon thereafter as the loyalty and security procedures should be successfully completed. In the ensuing days, additional personnel forms were sent to Dr. Williams as necessary, and a request was sent to the Civil Service Commission that the investigation be resumed. A full report was received from the Civil Service Commission on June 26, 1953.

In the interim, however, on June 15, 1953, the Executive Board of Unesco, meeting in Paris, had nominated Luther H. Evans to be Director General of Unesco, and on July 1, 1953, the General Conference confirmed the selection. On that date Dr. Evans resigned as Librarian of Congress, effective July 5, 1953. The President of the United States did not nominate a successor to the post of Librarian of Congress until April 1954. Meanwhile, the term of Dr. Evans' offer of an appointment to Dr. Williams expired in September 1953. Thus, the investigative report received on June 26, 1953, was never evaluated.

On April 22, 1954, President Eisenhower nominated L. Quincy Mumford of Cleveland, Ohio, to be Librarian of Congress; he was confirmed by the Senate on July 29, 1954, and took office on September 1, 1954. That month, a newspaper in London pub-

lished an article in which it was stated that the last poet
nominated to the Chair of Poetry "had failed to receive security
clearance," which implied that Dr. Williams had failed to meet
security requirements; a good deal of publicity in the American
press followed. On October 7, 1954, Librarian of Congress Mumford wrote Dr. Williams to assure him that he had not been
refused security clearance, that the investigative report had
never been evaluated, and that, although numerous questions on
the role and financing of the Chair of Poetry were outstanding,
the vacancy of the chair had no relation to Dr. Williams' security
status. On October 9, 1954, Dr. Williams wrote to the Librarian
to thank him for his kindness and to ask permission to publish
the letter. Permission was granted in a telephone call from the
Librarian to Dr. Williams on October 12 and in a confirming
telegram.

Although the Chair of Poetry in English had remained vacant
for four years, poetry in the Library of Congress had not been
permitted to languish, nor had the problem of arbiters been
settled. But new problems were current in plenty.

During the decade following Joseph Auslander's departure,
the generosity of Mrs. Gertrude Clark Whittall continued to
make itself manifest by various gifts of poetry and music manuscripts, as well as by additions to her earlier established Whittall Foundation for sponsoring chamber music. One of the ambi-
tions closest to her heart, allegedly first proposed to her by
Joseph Auslander, had been a Poetry Room with stained glass
windows. She continued to cherish this dream, but was able to
modify it in part when the "Poets' Room" was established on the
third floor "attic" of the Main Building, which she furnished, dis-
playing therein some of her best-loved Robinson manuscripts.

On November 27, 1950, she wrote the Librarian of Congress
that she wished to establish a Poetry Fund in the Library of
Congress, "the income from which is to be expended by the
Librarian of Congress for the development of the appreciation of
poetry in this country. Among the activities for which these
funds may be used are expenses connected with lectures on
poetry; public poetry readings; the service and upkeep of the
Poets' Corner [i.e., the present Poetry Room]; the publication of

bibliographies and other scholarly works designed to encourage the creation and appreciation of poetry, etc. These are to be regarded as suggestions but not limitations, and although I desire during my lifetime to be consulted on the choice of activities resulting from these gifts, I do not wish to impose any special conditions . . . ." Her offer was unanimously accepted by the Library of Congress Trust Fund Board on the recommendation of the Librarian, and at the next meeting, February 9-10, 1951, of the Fellows, her gift was announced on behalf of the Librarian by the Director of the Reference Department, Burton W. Adkinson, with "the suggestion that the formal inauguration of the program might be a reading of selections from Edwin Arlington Robinson's poems by an outstanding reader with commentary by a noted critic. Mr. Aiken has spoken with Professor Cleanth Brooks, of Yale University, who has made a selection of Robinson's poems and is available to appear with a reader if the proposal is adopted." (Minutes)

After considerable discussion emphasizing the preferability of having poets read their own poems, that primary attention should be given to "American Poetry of the present day," and that "the long range program should be under the direction of the Consultant in Poetry but that administrative detail should be delegated elsewhere, and that the Fellows could outline a program which successive Consultants could follow," the suggestion was approved with a further suggestion that in future "perhaps some of the income from the Whittall gift might be applied to fellowships."

At this meeting Mrs. Whittall entertained the Fellows with an elaborate luncheon and attended a reception given for them in the Poetry Room. All was charm and harmony, apparently, except for the possibilities inherent in the situation itself. On May 1, 1951, in the Library's Coolidge Auditorium, the inaugural program of the Gertrude Clark Whittall Poetry Fund presented a joint reading from the poems of Edwin Arlington Robinson by the well-known stage and screen actor, Burgess Meredith, and commentary by Fellow in American Letters Cleanth Brooks. It was a memorable evening from several points of view, and perhaps the shortest, as well as the best way to narrate it is to

quote in full two rather longish letters addressed to each of the
Fellows in advance of their convocation nearly a year later, in
February 1952. The first was Consultant Conrad Aiken's:

Dear
 The Consultant in Poetry thinks that along with the agenda for
the Fellows' meeting on February 29th, should go also some mention of a change in the status of the Consultant vis-a-vis the Whittall Poetry Fund and Poetry Program. In order that the Fellows
may be familiar with the facts, in advance of the meeting, I give a
brief summary of the events which have led up to this change.
Last spring, for the first of the programs under the Fund, it was
properly decided that in view of Mrs. Whittall's gifts of Housman
and Robinson manuscripts to the Library one of these should be
the subject of the first program: and it was agreed on all sides
that of these Robinson would be the more suitable. On the suggestion of the Consultant, Cleanth Brooks was invited to give the
lecture which was to accompany Burgess Meredith's reading, and
to select the poems to be read. But unexpected difficulties arose
over the question, raised initially by Mrs. Whittall, as to whether
portions of "Lancelot" should be included in the reading (this being one of Mrs. Whittall's gifts). It was the Consultant's feeling
that no pressure whatever should be put on Brooks, either to include the poem for reading, if he didn't so wish, or to comment
upon it; and accordingly the Consultant declined to act in the
matter. Brooks was nevertheless asked to include "Lancelot"— somewhat belatedly—and refused, on the ground that it didn't fit in
with what he had prepared to say, and wasn't anyway, a very
good poem. And that was that.
 Previous to all this, the Consultant had been asked for long-
range suggestions about the future programs, but more particularly with regard to the program for 1951-2, and in the summer,
while on vaction, in simultaneous letters to the Library and Mrs.
Whittall he outlined his idea for this: the establishment at the
Library of something comparable to the Charles Eliot Norton lectures at Harvard, with a national rather than merely local aim
and significance, and with the further specific proposal that the
first winter's program be a series of four lectures on twentieth

century American poetry, by decades, from 1910 to 1950. The
Consultant suggested that perhaps someone like R. P. Blackmur
be invited to give the lectures, and that readers comparable to
Burgess Meredith give illustrative readings. (Let it be said paren-
thetically that Mrs. Whittall was annoyed by the omission of
"Lancelot," and has a scunner on lectures, anyway!). But on his
return to the Library he was informed that it would perhaps be in
the best interests of all concerned if in future the administration
of the poetry programs be conducted by the Reference Department, rather than in the Poetry Room, but that, of course, the
Consultant would be kept informed of such decisions as were
taken, and such programs as were arranged. This has been the
situation ever since. The Reference Department, with the assistance of Mr. Waters, of the Music Division, administers the
program; and, in effect, the Consultant is no longer consulted. As
Dr. Evans has pointed out in his letter to the Fellows, this is
designed as a temporary measure. But I think, as in a sense a
precedent is thus being established, a statement by me is desirable at this point, in order that the Fellows may arrive at their own
views about it, and be in a position to discuss it at the meeting. It
is obviously an anomalous position that future Consultants will
inherit; one in which they will be *thought* to be responsible for
programs in which, in reality, they have no hand. It is certainly
not a prerogative of the Consultant to criticize the overall policies
of the Library. Yet this incumbent of the Chair would be less than
candid if he concealed his misgivings at seeing the Library, and in
the field of public relations, as this is, permitting its policy to be
shaped, at least partially, by one whose judgment in poetry is all
too lamentably betrayed by the books which she has provided for
the Poetry Room. (They are in my opinion, a disgrace!)

Yours sincerely,

Conrad Aiken
Chair of Poetry*

* Letter quoted by permission of Conrad Aiken.

The second letter emanated from the Director of the Reference Department:

Dear

In the light of matters presented in Mr. Aiken's letter to the Fellows in American Letters concerning the position of the Consultant in Poetry in relation to the program of readings supported by the Whittall Poetry Fund, I should like to present the Library administration's point of view on certain elements of the situation.

The library is obligated to consult Mrs. Whittall in the formulation of plans for the poetry readings which her generosity has made possible. In accepting Mrs. Whittall's gift the Library acceded to her stated wish that she be brought into the discussions relative to the selection of readers and of poems to be read. As for the character of the programs Mrs. Whittall has expressed a strong wish to have readings by well-known persons who are competent interpreters and who will attract public attention to this activity. She has stated a further wish that the readings be based, for the time being, on the works of famous poets of long-established reputation, which, in effect, rules out the contemporary period. Within this limitation there is, of course, a wide field for choice. Mrs. Whittall particularly wished not to pattern the program around a series of lectures on poetry. As Dr. Evans has stated in his letter to you, the Library has agreed to follow Mrs. Whittall's wishes.

The Library administration considers Mr. Aiken's proposal for lectures by Professor Blackmur, with illustrative readings by persons comparable to Burgess Meredith, to be an excellent one. It has been considered carefully and will be given further attention for the long-range program. The wide difference between Mrs. Whittall's wishes and Mr. Aiken's idea of the direction the program should follow placed the Library in the position of having to break a tie, as there appeared to be no middle-ground for compromise. I wish to make it clear that in reaching its decision the Library was firmly of the opinion first, that a successful program of readings could be launched by the plan adopted, and second, that the plan would permit a desirable flexibility in the form of individual programs.

We recognize the position in which this places Mr. Aiken and we would have welcomed a situation in which a decision congenial to all interested parties could have been made. However, in the face of the wide differences of opinion it appeared to be entirely logical to place the administration of the program in the Reference Department Office rather than to impose upon Mr. Aiken concern with the details of a plan with which he was not in sympathy and which he considered to be incompatible with his Consultantship. The Library has complete respect for Mr. Aiken's views and it seeks his continued advice on the readings to be given on the present plan and his ideas on the long-range program. I have discussed these questions with Mr. Aiken and I can state that his counsel is needed and welcomed by the Library administration. The poetry readings have only started and a great deal of thought must be given to their future. The Library has made no commitment that would prevent a departure from the current pattern.

In engaging theatrical notables to read, the Library does not attempt to control the selection of poems to be read. Much may depend upon the taste and repertoire of the readers. The programs are developed in discussion, or by correspondence, between the readers and the Library and neither the Consultant nor the Library exerts pressure in the selections. The readers are far more free in making their selections, in fact, than are the chamber music groups in choosing compositions for performance in the Coolidge Auditorium. In this, admittedly, the Consultant in Poetry now has comparatively little opportunity to function.

The instance concerning the Robinson reading and "Lancelot" arose entirely from Mrs. Whittall's extreme concern at not having been consulted in the selections and at the omission of poems of which she had presented the manuscripts to the Library. The program selected by Mr. Aiken and Professor Brooks had been accepted without question by the Library. Mrs. Whittall's insistent inquiries were the cause of a call to Professor Brooks to inform him of the problem and to ask his opinion of a substitution from "Lancelot," *not* to ask him to change the program against his judgment. Professor Brooks stated his reasons for disapproving the substitution and was told that the program would not be changed. There was no intention of asserting pressure and Professor Brooks gave no indication at the time that he interpreted the inquiry in that light.

Sincerely,

Burton W. Adkinson
Director, Reference Department*

Although the meeting on February 29 and March 1 had before it a full and potentially fruitful agenda, including recommendation of a successor to Conrad Aiken as Consultant, the election of new Fellows, the desirability of limiting tenure of Fellows, the establishment of endowed fellowships, ways of improving the Library's acquisition of papers of contemporary writers, and the future management of the Whittall Poetry Fund, the bulk of attention on Friday the 29th was devoted to the last of these, with the result that the Fellows adopted the following Resolution.

> The present confusion between the Reference Department and the Consultant in Poetry in the administration of the funds for the poetry programs seems to the Fellows deplorable. It seems to them that the Consultant should have a decisive voice in all such matters, especially when, in the public view, he is held responsible. If he can not have a decisive voice in any particular program, it should be clearly announced that the program is being given under other auspices. In any case, there should be consultation between the Library and a committee of the Fellows with the principle in mind that, if there is to be a Consultant in Poetry, he should be concerned with the administration of any permanent poetry funds. (Minutes)

On the following day, the bulk of the debate devolved from the Librarian's acceptance of the resolution. The discussion sought

* Letter quoted by permission of Burton Adkinson.

ways of implementing it, and the conclusion was that a committee of Fellows would be the best means. They would act as liaison between Mrs. Whittall, the Consultant, and the Library Administration, in order to educate the donor concerning the best possible uses of the Fund. The one item on the agenda which the Librarian's letter of transmittal prior to the meeting had stressed as his primary hope for some years past, "that the Consultant and Fellows would play an active role in the program for acquiring manuscripts of publications and the personal papers of important American literary figures," received only nominal and inconclusive discussion. But the item concerning Consultant Aiken's proposal of endowed fellowships received lengthy discussion and enthusiastic endorsement. A succinct summary of the Library Administration's reaction to this proposal and somewhat indicative, perhaps, of feeling about the meeting as a whole was a comment penned on a slip of paper appended to the file under date of May 7, 1952: "This is so goofy I am tempted to file and forget . . . . "

Such was pretty much the state of affairs when the writer of this account assumed his position of Chief, General Reference and Bibliography Division, in the fall of 1952, with the Poetry Office and the operation of programs under the Whittall Poetry Fund not the least of his assigned responsibilities. With neither the advice of a Consultant in Poetry, nor an inkling of the intentions of Librarian Evans in regard to the future of the Fellows in American Letters, the work of the Poetry Office and the arrangement of programs under the Whittall Poetry Fund was carried on chiefly by dint of able staff work on the part of Miss Phyllis Armstrong, the Special Assistant in Poetry, who had demonstrated since 1946 her ability to perform yeoman service under a succession of Consultants, as well as in liaison with the donor of the Poetry Fund. Administrative responsibility for the activities of the Poetry Office and the programs carried on under the auspices of the Whittall Poetry and Literature Fund continued to be under the writer's direct supervision, from 1952 until this writing.

Planning programs under the Whittall Fund, in consultation

with the donor, was a perennial challenge that proved not un-
fruitful, considering that the increments which Mrs. Whittall
added from time to time during the next decade, up to her death
in 1965 at age 98, swelled the total endowment in the Fund to
more than $900,000. For one whose love of poetry was first
stimulated, as she once confided, by an early girlhood gift of a
copy of Bulwer-Lytton's *Lucile,* her taste in poetry was by no
means as atrocious as it was purported. She preferred
Shakespeare above all and admitted to liking E. A. Robinson and
A. E. Housman best among her contemporaries, although
Robert Frost held for her a personal charm as well as poetic
stature. Of the "younger" poets, whom the Fellows in American
Letters for the most part had represented, she admitted no liking, but she agreed readily enough that "her programs" should
not ignore them. In the course of the ensuing decade, as the
"younger" poets appeared more and more frequently under her
auspices, as it were, she studied their works beforehand and in
every instance made perceptive observations, not merely on
their qualities as poets, but on their frequent deficiencies as
readers of their own best pieces. To the present, more than half a
hundred living poets have been presented to Library of Congress audiences under the auspices of the Whittall Fund, and
many of their readings have been broadcast by educational radio
stations across the country.

Mrs. Whittall continued, however, to prefer Shakespeare and
"classics" of English and American literature when read by
professionals of stage and rostrum. Thus many notable performances and readings were brought to the Library by the elite of
the stage: e. g., Charles Laughton, Fredric March, Arnold Moss,
Emlyn Williams—for Mrs. Whittall preferred male readers and
gave a good argument that their voices were simply better instru-
ments for poetry. Nevertheless, she agreed to include Margaret
Webster, Dorothy Stickney, and Florence Eldridge, among many
others. The heyday of staged readings seems to have passed, but
who knows when they may return, as they have more than once, to
stimulate audiences of a new generation to the love of poetry, for
which Gertrude Clark Whittall primarily dedicated her gift?

Perhaps more far-reaching in some respects has been the series of lectures presented and published under auspices of the Whittall Fund. While in no sense an effort to compete with or duplicate the purposes of such famed series as the Harvard Norton Lectures, the Whittall Lectures have found their place in American Letters along with the annual lectures of the incumbent Consultant in Poetry. Thus Mrs. Whittall's interests and those enunciated by the Fellows in American Letters came into close if not exact proximity in the course of time. But what of the Fellows themselves?

Following their meeting of February 29– March 1, 1952, some of the recommendations which the Librarian had been "tempted to file and forget," and subsequent developments in the appointment of William Carlos Williams as Consultant, there was a hiatus of nearly a year during which there was understandably some reluctance to convoke the Fellows in official meeting. Whereupon a few of them convoked themselves, at Conrad Aiken's suggestion, in New York City in a "rump meeting," on Saturday, April 11, 1953. On the following Wednesday, Aiken visited the Library to discuss their deliberations with Librarian Evans, but in his absence reported to the writer of this account that the Fellows present at the meeting felt they were being "allowed to die on the vine" and were considering the desirability of resigning.

During these discussions an effort was made to clarify the administrative problem of not being able to understand just what continuing function there could be for the Fellows, under the circumstances, beyond that of merely advising the Library, and that there had seemed long since a disposition on their part to conceive their function as perhaps something more than this. The first necessity seemed to be to define the function of the Fellows so that areas of difference with Library officers could be minimized, if not entirely eliminated. It also seemed obvious that until a Consultant in Poetry was actively on duty nothing much could be accomplished. On the following day, Aiken repaired to his former desk in the Poetry Room and wrote the absent Librarian as follows:

Poetry Room
April 16, 1953

Dear Luther:

I'm extremely sorry to have missed you, for there was much that I wanted to discuss with you, on behalf of the Fellows, or semi-officially so—we held a rump meeting last Saturday in New York, and as I was coming to Washington *anyway*, it was thought useful if I could talk with you. Warren, Adams, Bogan, Brooks, Florence Williams, and myself were present, and the entire situation of the Fellows, vis-a-vis the Library, was considered at length. We all, to begin with, felt relieved by the turn of events in the case of Williams, and were delighted with your letter of April 2nd (?) to him, setting the clearance process in action: we agreed that this was a happy termination of an unfortunate business, and were also glad to hear from Mrs. Williams that Williams is now quite rejuvenated.

But we were all also agreed in thinking that the position of the Fellows leaves something to be desired. We feel that a meeting ought to have been called, and all the more so because of the difficulties about the Consultant, and we feel that one should *now* be called as soon as possible: either this spring or early summer, or perhaps in September, as between the 15th and 25th, when those who are teachers usually have a slack period: this date, in general, was thought to be perhaps better than February. It was thought that the whole function of the Fellows needed to be reconsidered and defined, and that in some sense the Library, while perhaps not abusing us, was at any rate not properly *using* us, and we would like an opportunity of assuring you that this is something we mean. The questions of endowed Fellowships and the manuscript collection were both examined at length, particularly the latter, and with a feeling that more could have been done than *has* been done; but, as I myself pointed out, the lag here was more the Library's fault than our own, for my own letters of request still lie mouldering somewhere in the Lower Depths. But many suggestions were here forthcoming, and a complete unanimity on the notion that there were a great many such matters which could more properly be held over for a real meeting. The poetry programs were considered too, and some anxiety expressed as to whether the spirit of our resolution of last year was being observed—but of this, in the absence of a Consultant, we of course knew little. And finally, there was general agreement that if it were possible, prior to such a meeting of the Fellows, we would all very much like to have you come to New York for a dinner-meeting of such of the Fellows as we can get together, for a more personal pow-wow about all these things. We are aware, as you too must be, of some of the "tensions" that exist between the Library and the Fellows, we feel that some of these, if not all, may be administrational or due to mutual misunderstanding, and we think that at this juncture a more personal approach might be helpful. If you could let me know at Brewster, Massachusetts, after April 25th, of a possible date in New York, I would set things in motion, or perhaps better still you could ask Miss Armstrong, who has all the addresses, to set about it. Finally, I should add that at this rump meeting Brooks was more or less speaking for Auden, and myself for Eliot, with whom I had discussed it in London.

I lunched yesterday, very pleasantly, with Adkinson, Basler and Gooch, and put before them some of all this, as I thought it desirable that they too should know what was on our minds. On the subject of manuscript collections it seemed to me there has been a real misunderstanding of our position, due, I think, to the remarks of Thornton Wilder—the rest of us differ from him, and Warren in particular had some excellent ideas on the subject, i. e., periodic exhibits *tied in* with talks—for example, as I suggested last spring, a loan exhibit of John Gould Fletcher, to which we could invite Mrs. Charlie May Fletcher for commentary. And last of all, in another connection, Basler having said that he had not wanted to proceed with Huntington Cairns *in re* a Bollingen grant for recordings, without the backing of a Consultant, I volunteered (perhaps out of turn) to come down and serve in this capacity for a few days, if it were deemed suitable *and* I could have my expenses! (I talked with Huntington Cairns at the Bollingen Foundation a few weeks ago, and he said he had been prepared to go ahead with it at last October's meeting, but that the memoranda had not been sent to him. He still seemed to think the thing could be done.)

And I think that about covers it.

With affectionate regards,

Conrad Aiken*

* Letter quoted by permission of Conrad Aiken.

Librarian Evans pondered these possibilities and replied on May 12 that he was sorry to have been absent when Aiken called and that he hoped for an opportunity to talk again in the near future about the interesting questions raised in Aiken's letter. He felt, however, that these matters should wait until the Williams case had been cleared up and the Consultant was on the job and available to participate.

There the matter rested for more than two years. Librarian L. Quincy Mumford, who succeeded Luther Evans, was confronted by numerous problems upon his assumption of office, September 1, 1954, and quite understandably perhaps was in no hurry to pick up immediately all the "hot potatoes" which had been left in the Library's oven. There were many serious conferences on administrative levels of what action to take in regard to the Fellows and the Consultant in Poetry, and when to take it. Consensus was reached in August 1955 that a Consultant should be appointed as soon as possible, and that the advice of the Fellows in American Letters should be sought. In the interim, the term of appointment (limited to seven years by their own Resolution in 1951) of several Fellows had expired, including that of Conrad Aiken, the most active among them. Nevertheless, it was decided to include Aiken and a few other former Fellows among those to whom the Librarian would address a letter summarizing the status quo and asking their advice concerning the appointment of a Consultant in Poetry and the future of the Fellows in American Letters. The letter as drafted read as follows:

Dear

Mr. Conrad Aiken, whose term as Fellow in American Letters expired in August, 1954, but whose interest in the Library continues, has represented to me on several occasions the collective interest of the Fellows in the arrangement of a meeting at the Library of Congress. Mr. Aiken has been informed that the Library has no funds available to cover the travel expenses of the Fellows as formerly, 31 USC 673 expressly prohibiting the use of public monies for the compensation or expenses "of any commission, council, board or other similar body, or any members there-

of . . . . unless the creation of the same shall be or shall have
been authorized by law," and there being no gift fund which can
be reasonably construed as providing for such exigencies. In a
letter dated April 23, 1955, Mr. Aiken expressed the belief that a
quorum of the Fellows would be willing to meet in Washington at
their own expense. Naturally, I hesitate to ask the Fellows to
assume this expense of time as well as money, and I have therefore decided to summarize my thinking concerning the status and
function of the Fellows as well as the appointment of a Consultant and to ask your comment and advice in writing.

A study of the records reveals that the Fellows in American
Letters were conceived and first appointed to advise the formulation of policies governing the collections and services of the
Library in regard to phonograph recordings of American poets
and the acquisition of manuscripts and books of American
authors. The minutes of the first meeting of the Fellows in May,
1944, record a full discussion of these activities and a list of
recommendations submitted to the Librarian of Congress. During succeeding years, under the direction of Mr. Allen Tate and
his successors as Consultant in Poetry, some attention was given
to the matter of acquisition of books and manuscripts. Results
appear to have been slight, and the matter was again brought to
the attention of the Fellows by the Librarian in the last meeting
held, February 29 – March 1, 1952. The Consultant, Mr. Aiken,
shortly thereafter drafted a letter for use in soliciting manuscripts, and a program of increased effort was formulated, to be
carried out by his successor.

In the matter of recording living poets reading their own works,
considerably more progress was effected. With the assistance of
two grants from the Bollingen Foundation, under the direct
supervision of the Consultant in Poetry, advised by the Fellows,
the albums of "Twentieth Century Poetry in English," Series I
and Series II, were issued by the Library. The reception of these
recordings by the press and by the public has been very gratifying.

Because of a series of circumstances with which you are
familiar to some extent, the Library has been without a Consultant in Poetry since Mr. Aiken's second appointment terminated
three years ago. In consequence, we have not been able to continue as actively as is desirable in the development of recordings
of additional poets and in re-recording poets already issued in

Series I and Series II for ampler representation on Long Playing Records.

In view of the foregoing considerations, I propose to appoint a Consultant in Poetry who can actively assist in the development of plans for recording and issuing further poetry records and who can undertake to supervise the selection of poets, the process of recording, and the preparation of the new records. Although this is the most immediate need, the matter of the Library's acquisition of manuscripts should also receive attention, and there are numerous opportunities for consultation on literary matters which, as in the past, continue to make the absence of the Poetry Consultant felt.

I would therefore appreciate your sending me the names of one or more candidates whom you would recommend for appointment as Consultant, to take office this fall for one year, with the possibility of renewing this appointment for a second year. I recognize that it may not be possible to fill the appointment this fall or for a full year, and, if such is the case, I will consider making an interim appointment until such time as a desirable appointment can be made. I am also asking for recommendations from the other Fellows and from a few other persons.

There is the further question concerning the future of the Fellows on which I should like to have your comment and advice. As now appears, I do not foresee any possibility of profitably reactivating the meetings of the Fellows in the Library of Congress on the basis of available resources. There is thus also a question as to the utility of making new appointments of Fellows in American Letters. Mr. Aiken has on several occasions during the last two years represented that the Fellows as a group feel their association with the Library of Congress has been fruitless and pointless. I must confess that this feeling, together with a considerable sense of frustration that it should be so, seems to be held by the several administrative officers of the Library with whom I have discussed the problem. Although we have collectively given no little thought to this state of affairs, we have not been able on our part to formulate any more meaningful or more frequent matters on which to consult. For this reason I am hesitant to consider making new appointments to replace Mr. Aiken, Mr. Auden, and Mr. T. S. Eliot, whose seven-year terms expired in the fall of last year.

It has been suggested that when the Chair of Poetry has been filled and regularly maintained again, consultation by correspondence and personal conference with individual authors, both present and past incumbents of the Fellowship, as well as other authors, might be carried on through the Consultant equally well without benefit of formal appointment of additional Fellows. This would mean that upon the expiration of the respective seven-year terms of each of the present incumbents the formal appointments would lapse and thereafter the Library would seek suggestions and advice from the literary profession on an ad hoc basis.

Your views on these several proposals will be greatly appreciated.

Sincerely yours,

By mid-November replies had come in from six of the ten Fellows, as well as a number of other literary persons who had been asked by the Librarian to recommend candidates for the Consultantship in Poetry. Few poets were nominated by more than one person, and the Fellows' replies, in particular, dodged the question, some commenting that this should be arrived at by discussion, as in the past, rather than by letter. On this point, as well as several others, Fellow Archibald MacLeish's reply undertook to provide the Librarian background, as well as advice from the fountainhead, as it were.

September 2, 1955

Dear Quincy:

I had been told that the question of the Fellows in American Letters was up for consideration and that you were giving it considerable thought. I can well understand your concern and I am grateful for an opportunity to comment.

More important than any of the specific questions you raise in your letter of the 31st August is the general background. The Fellows were appointed in the first place not so much to perform specific tasks as to bring the Library into some kind of contact with the practise of the art of letters as distinguished from the

record of that practise. In 1939 (I cannot speak of the situation
prior to that time but I think it safe to assume it was the same)
the Library of Congress had no relationship whatever with the
living culture (music excepted and maybe etchings!) of the country. Most writers thought of it as a museum and the Library
reciprocated in kind. Few living American writers were adequately represented in its collections outside the standard names
and the standard works. Contemporary poetry was largely
neglected except for the names familiar to the anthologists. There
was no serious effort to collect literary manuscripts. There was
no effort whatever to bring American writers to the Principal
American Library as it was sometimes called. Historians aside,
they were rarely seen there. And, Washington being what it is,
nothing in the District made good the lack. I don't need to remind
you of my deep devotion and unmitigated admiration for the L. of
C. but despite those emotions I was keenly aware at that time, as
were many of our colleagues, that the Library was a very paro-
chial and provincial place for all its vast collections. It touched the
American present only through the American past and not very
adequately at that. The conversation at the Librarian's Round
Table had to be heard to be believed—and was hardly believable
even so. In fact I believed in it so little that I found it very hard to
go.

Believing as I did and do that Libraries are something more
than cold storage plants, and having a particular interest in the
living culture of the country and especially in the living art of
poetry and letters I attempted to correct the situation I have
described as well as I could. I pried the chair of poetry out from
under Joe Auslander who looked upon himself as proprietor and
put it on an annual basis so as to bring to the Library a sequence
of first class writers. It's an impressive list by and large. Some
mistakes but not many. I then set up the Fellowship in American
Letters with a view to giving the Library the benefit of the
presence from time to time, as well as the counsel, of the country's foremost living writers. There was no attempt to "write up"
the job in specific terms because it was the contact, the association, which was desired, but the specific suggestions were those
you mentioned—above all help in building up the collections and
in securing manuscripts. As I don't need to tell you, the L of C is

at a great disadvantage in comparison with a Library like Harvard's because it has no faculty of eminent scholars to ride herd on its collecting policy. The Chief Assistant Librarian when I went to Washington used to order books by the feel in the seat of his pants. He had never, so far as I know, read a contemporary book of any kind—certainly never a book of verse. I don't want to be unfair to Mr. [Martin A.] Roberts who was in many ways a noble man but it was a Hell of a way to run a railroad. Verner [Clapp] can tell you some stories that will make your hair rise.

The venture was never as successful as I hoped it would be. For one thing it was my baby and I was out of the Library a great deal in 1944 when it got under way, and left for good in December of that year. But no one will doubt I think—certainly no one who was familiar with the status quo ante, that it was successful. Some of our colleagues found the Fellows hard to handle: writers are apt to be mavericks. But the position of the Library in the eyes of cultivated men and women here and abroad was decidedly improved. The serious collection of literary manuscripts was undertaken. The recording program—about which I have reservations, largely because concerns like Caedmon make so much better records—accomplished a great deal. And, whatever the disappointments on the collection front the Library need not now blush for its American holdings.

I don't know what you ought to do. If the Library can't pay the expenses of necessary consultants who are willing to give their time (which seems to me a shocking fact) you have little choice. I would express only one opinion: that you ought in some way to hold the gains made in the brief years in which the Fellows flourished. It would be tragic if the country's national library and the country's writers drifted back into the condition of mutual disinterest which obtained fifteen years ago.

And I would proffer only one piece of advice: if you are going to liquidate the Fellows, as you imply, do by all means call a meeting of the present and immediately past members and give them a chance to be heard. Such a meeting could take place in New York which most of your Fellows could reach far more easily at their own cost than Washington. I urge this for the sake of the Library not for the sake of the Fellows.

One thing that meeting should do is to talk about the next incumbent of the chair of poetry. Making nominations without a chance to discuss is a pretty unsatisfactory proceeding as you will agree.

best to you all

Archie*

Accepting the suggestion of a meeting in New York, Librarian Mumford wrote a letter to each Fellow, offering to meet on one of five possible dates in December. Only two of the replies indicated the possibility of attendance—Professors R. P. Blackmur and Cleanth Brooks—and plans for a meeting were abandoned.

Whatever impression MacLeish, and perhaps others, may have received of an intention to "liquidate the Fellows," this was not precisely the case. Rather, the Library administration collectively was at something of a loss as to how to use them. Conrad Aiken's phrasing two years earlier, that "the Library, while perhaps not *abusing* us, was at any rate not properly *using* us," remained apropos, albeit somewhat one-sided. One thing was clear, and had been for many months, that until a Consultant in Poetry was on duty at the Library, liaison with the literary world would have much to be desired.

In the absence of a convocation of Fellows, where customarily the question of whom to appoint had been resolved, more or less informally, by knowledgeable discussion of what poet among those qualified might most deserve appointment, and also be currently "available" to accept the post, the Librarian could no longer merely accept the one thus chosen. He had to choose and appoint his choice from among the many whose names came recommended highly but by no means unanimously, not merely by Fellows but by a considerable number of other unofficial representatives of the literary community. The first Consultant thus appointed was Randall Jarrell, who reported for duty in September 1956. He would remain upon invitation for an optional second year. Beginning with Jarrell, Consultants served

* Letter quoted by permission of Archibald MacLeish.

for one or two years, depending largely on the poet's wishes. For both the poet and the Library administration, the second year gained much from the experience of the first. Perhaps a listing of the later Consultants and their term of office would not be amiss at this point in the narrative, for the reader's convenience:

Randall Jarrell	—	1956-1958
Robert Frost	—	1958-1959
Richard Eberhart	—	1959-1961
Louis Untermeyer	—	1961-1963
Howard Nemerov	—	1963-1964
Reed Whittemore	—	1964-1965
Stephen Spender	—	1965-1966
James Dickey	—	1966-1968
William Jay Smith	—	1968-1970
William Stafford	—	1970-1971
Josephine Jacobsen	—	1971-1973

One of Consultant Jarrell's first assignments was to study the history of the Fellows and make recommendations concerning the future of the group. His memorandum of recommendations dated November 20, 1956, pointed out that although the Fellows of the Library of Congress in American Letters had served the Library in an advisory capacity with relation to their particular fields of knowledge, and advised the Library concerning the development of its collections and the promotion of its services of American literary materials, Librarian Evans, in 1952, had felt that these functions might be somewhat more clearly defined. Jarrell agreed and suggested further that, as the Fellows had not met since 1952, and as there were only seven of them left, it might seem advisable for the Library to consider the functions that the Fellows had or might have, and weigh the advantages or disadvantages to the Library of the continued existence of the group.

He thought the main disadvantage to be obvious: since the Fellows were an autonomous or semi-autonomous group with standards that were not, necessarily, the Library's, it had been possible for them to take actions that had been either publicly (as in the case of Pound) or privately (as in the case of the administration of the Whittall Poetry Fund) embarrassing to the Library. He believed, however, that if the Fellows were a more varied and more widely representative group, this disadvantage would be minimized. It was because the Fellows had been a specialized, homogeneous body of poets and critics that they had tended to act, sometimes, in a specialized way, and if the Fellows could be made more truly representative of the variety of American literature and art and thought, they might reflect more exactly what seemed to be the original motives for the appointing of fellows and honorary consultants.

It was therefore his suggestion that the Librarian consider appointing a number of new Fellows, giving a wider representation to the different fields of literature, and assuring the Library of a genuinely representative group of Fellows that would be more distinguished, more useful, and from the Library's point of view, a great deal safer.

The memorandum continued with a lengthy discussion of the activities which Jarrell believed, in concurrence with Librarian Evans or the Fellows, or both, to be potentially of "the greatest benefit to the Library": namely, assistance in the acquisition of papers of literary persons, in improving the acquisition of foreign literature, in obtaining endowments, in establishing a lecture series and in selecting lecturers, readers, and above all the Consultant in Poetry. He concluded with the observation that the Fellows were the Government's only official connection with literature, and that their existence made apparent to everyone the Library's interest in, and concern for, American literature.

Librarian Mumford did not take action on Jarrell's recommendations until August 16, 1957, when he addressed a letter to those Fellows whose appointments were still in effect or had only recently expired—five in all: Elizabeth Bishop, R. P. Blackmur, Cleanth Brooks, John Crowe Ransom, and Thornton Wilder. The letter explained that the Library continued to have no funds that could be used to finance meetings, but that the Consultant in Poetry felt his work would be greatly facilitated if he had a panel of persons distinguished in American letters upon whom he might call for advice and assistance. Also explained was the intention to convert all the Library's fellows, honorary consultants, and experts to a uniform title of Honorary Consultant, with a term of three years.# Jarrell's proposed activities for the Honorary Consultants in American Letters were outlined and the hope expressed that each Fellow addressed would accept a further appointment with the new title. On August 21, a similar letter offering appointment went to Maxwell Anderson, James Gould Cozzens, William Faulkner, and Eudora Welty. Of the former group, Miss Bishop and Messrs Blackmur, Brooks, and Ransom accepted; of the latter group, Maxwell Anderson and Eudora Welty. Announcement of their respective appointments was made on December 19, 1957.

The Fellows in American Letters and the Honorary Consultants in American Letters, with their respective terms of appointment, are as follows. The obvious overlapping of names in both lists is accounted for by the decision to convert all Fellows to Honorary Consultants in 1957.

FELLOWS IN AMERICAN LETTERS

Leonie Adams	1949-1956
Conrad Aiken	1947-1954
Wystan Hugh Auden	1947-1954
Elizabeth Bishop	1952-1956
Richard P. Blackmur	1952-1956
Louise Bogan	1946-1951
Cleanth Brooks	1952-1956
Van Wyck Brooks	1944-1946
Katherine Garrison Chapin	1944-1953
Thomas Stearns Eliot	1947-1954
Paul Green	1944-1953
Robert Lowell	1949-1956
Archibald MacLeish	1949-1956
Samuel Eliot Morison	1950-1956
Katherine Anne Porter	1944-1953
John Crowe Ransom	1950-1956
Carl Sandburg	1944-1946
Karl Shapiro	1947-1953
Theodore Spencer	1947-1949*
Allen Tate	1944-1951
Willard Thorp	1944-1951
Mark Van Doren	1944-1945

Funds became available a few months later to cover expenses of a meeting, and a convocation was set for April 18 and 19, 1958. Of the six Honorary Consultants, four were able to attend—

Robert Penn Warren	1945-1953
Thornton Wilder	1950-1956
William Carlos Williams	1949-1956

HONORARY CONSULTANTS IN AMERICAN LETTERS

Conrad Aiken	1968-1974
Maxwell Anderson	1957-1959*
Saul Bellow	1963-1966
Elizabeth Bishop	1957-1960
Richard P. Blackmur	1957-1964
Catherine Drinker Bowen	1961-1967
Cleanth Brooks	1957-1964
Katherine Garrison Chapin	1966-1972
Babette Deutsch	1961-1967
James Dickey	1968-1974
Richard Eberhart	1963-1969
Ralph Ellison	1966-1972
Josephine Jacobsen	1973-
MacKinlay Kantor	1967-1973
Clare Booth Luce	1973-
Bernard Malamud	1972-
James Michener	1973-
Marianne Moore	1967-1973
Howard Nemerov	1964-1970
Katherine Anne Porter	1963-1969
John Crowe Ransom	1957-1960
Elmer Rice	1963-1966
William Jay Smith	1970-
William Stafford	1971-
John Steinbeck	1963-1966
William Styron	1972-
Louis Untermeyer	1961-1967
John Updike	1972-
Robert Penn Warren	1966-1972
Eudora Welty	1957-1964
John Hall Wheelock	1967-1973
Reed Whittemore	1965-1971

* Died before completing term.

Messrs. Brooks, Blackmur, and Ransom, and Miss Welty. Items
on the agenda included 1) extension of the program of recording
readings for the archive—for which a new grant had been obtained from the Bollingen Foundation, 2) obtaining additional
funds to permit issuance of a new series of records for sale, 3)
the desirability and possibility of obtaining funds to endow an
annual lecture series, 4) acquisition of literary manuscripts and
personal papers of authors, 5) improving the acquisition of
European books, 6) the preparation of annotated bibliographies,
7) the continuing program and duties of the Consultant in
Poetry, and 8) the continuing role of the Honorary Consultants
in American Letters.

The meeting proved to be a most cordial exchange of views
and offering of advice and suggestions. On the topic concerning
the future usefulness of the Honorary Consultants, everyone
seemed to agree, and it was specifically recognized that one of
the main functions of the Consultant in Poetry should be to keep
the Honorary Consultants informed of developments and to
solicit their suggestions, whether in convocation or by personal
and official communication.

Although consensus seemed relatively complete and practically all of the suggestions were carried forward during the
next few years, the extent to which continuing liaison and communication was maintained by each of Jarrell's successors is not
readily assessable. It is safe to say, however, that the degree has
varied considerably in direct relation to the personal inclina-
tions of each Consultant in Poetry beginning with Robert Frost,
who was certainly more inclined to give advice than to ask it! In
any event, no further convocations of the Honorary Consultants
would be called for the next eight years, although the various individuals continued to give invaluable assistance by correspondence and telephone to the Consultant in Poetry and to the
Librarian of Congress and to this writer in his overall responsibility for the affairs of the Poetry Office, as well as for the
programs arranged under the Whittall Fund. That once so
touchy subject had been, and continued to remain, solved more
or less satisfactorily, by a mutual understanding that whatever

the Consultant in Poetry wished to propose would be arranged, insofar as possible.

Each Consultant in Poetry has brought his or her own personal impact to bear, not only on the Library of Congress, but also on the nation's capital at large, and each should have his own story told, as the writer has tried to tell Robert Frost's in a separate narrative, "Yankee Vergil." Although the scope of the present narrative does not permit this, three events in recent years stand out as deserving special mention among the many noteworthy readings, lectures and dramatic productions presented by the Library of Congress: the National Poetry Festival, October 22-24, 1962; the Symposium on The Little Magazine and Contemporary Literature, April 2 and 3, 1965; and the International Poetry Festival, April 13-15, 1970.

A National Poetry Festival had been considered for several years as an appropriate recognition by the Library of Congress, not only of the numerous poets who had served as Consultant and/or Fellow, but of the remarkable burgeoning of American poetry in general during the first half of the twentieth century, continuing from, if not actually beginning with, the establishment of Harriet Monroe's *Poetry, A Magazine of Verse* in 1912. The approaching fiftieth anniversary of that event seemed to afford an especially appropriate date, and the presence of Consultant in Poetry Louis Untermeyer, whose anthologies had done yeoman service in making modern poetry more widely known, left but one ingredient missing—financial assistance. Once again the Bollingen Foundation agreed to pick up the tab, and plans went forward.

Although a number of poets were unable to accept the invitation to participate and a few were prevented at the last moment for various reasons, twenty-nine poets and two critics took part in the three-day program, comprised of symposiums, readings, and lectures. In addition, more than fifty poets attended and participated in the discussions, which, like the readings and lectures, were opened to the public. Not even the occurrence of the Cuban Missile Crisis in the midst of the Festival could dampen the spirit of poetry. The cancellation of plans for a White House reception for the poets brought a measure of disappointment, however, and the press paid little attention to this notable literary event, perhaps, or at least one hopes, because of the "crisis." The Festival *Proceedings* were published by the Library of Congress in 1964 and received wide distribution.

Organized by Consultant in Poetry Reed Whittemore, the Symposium on The Little Magazine and Contemporary Literature, April 2 and 3, 1965, was financed by a grant from the Carnegie Corporation. Far from honorific in purpose, and certainly more explosive in its discussions, the Symposium made its point, not only about the nation's indebtedness to little magazines as hotbeds of literary talent, but also about their comparative neglect at the hands of the public and the sources of support. Consultant Whittemore summarized his impressions of his handiwork in a Foreword to the *Symposium*, published for the Library of Congress in 1966 by the Modern Language Association of America:

> It was hoped that from this group some worthwhile proposals would float forth for redeeming or restoring to health a kind of publishing now, it seems evident, in real trouble. This hope was not realized. Though a number of proposals were in fact made — I, for example, made a perfectly magnificent one — none seemed to take hold. Most participants left the conference persuaded of the difficulties of joint efforts at restoration and mightily impressed by the extraordinary absence of agreement.
>
> It was an exciting meeting. Maybe the disagreements are in themselves instructive. "Back to the drawing boards," cry the world's architects when their roofs leak, their bridges fall down. The architects of little magazines can now go back to their drawing boards too—and perhaps project another conference. (*The Little Magazine and Contemporary Literature*, p. vi)

Consultant Whittemore did not mention that the Symposium achieved an historic "first" when the Coolidge Auditorium of the Library of Congress reverberated to the sound of four letter words as discussion of their appropriateness to literary expression became explicit. That fact alone might have suggested the appropriateness of the imprimature of the Modern Language Association of America on the publication of the *Symposium* in

toto (1966), had not administrative decisions prompted the identical outcome, once the Association agreed to accept the tran-
script for publication.

Whittemore's term as Consultant illustrated in other ways the
difficulty encountered to some extent by each Consultant in
precisely defining the role he should play as representative of
the world of letters in the nation's capital. It would seem that
governments today can't use poets as poets. St.-John Perse and
Archibald MacLeish were not really exceptions, for although
they most certainly were used by their governments, they were
not used as poets. And Robert Frost is the example of perfect
failure in this respect. His "sovereign" not only couldn't use him
after the inaugural but even, it is reliably reported, got a bit
worried by Frost's persistent availability.

Whittemore was very good humored about this failure of ours,
so far as it affected him, and publicly recommended in a lecture
at the Library of Congress that the post of Consultant in Poetry
be abolished in "a world in which the creative intelligence has no
role in the world's affairs," except of course the role "to record
that observation and go to bed."

Whittemore's conviction that the United States government
should be able to use a few poets *as poets* in Washington seemed
so obviously true that the writer began to feel like a character in
Garson Kanin's movie, "Some Kind of a Nut," when invited to a
meeting in the Library's Poetry Room, along with several government officials of some status, to discuss that possibility. The
reader can guess easily enough the predictable results, but a
good deal of imagination and sympathy will be required to esti-
mate the peculiar sense of humor necessary to one who agrees
with the proposition and still sits through the protracted discussion.

Although first proposed by Consultant Stephen Spender in
1966, the International Poetry Festival, April 13-15, 1970, had
been delayed until the term of Consultant William Jay Smith,
largely because exploration of possible sources of financial support had proved negative. The Bollingen Foundation, several
times benefactor of and collaborator in the Library's literary
projects, had announced suspension of its grants-in-aid program

in 1966, and no other foundation came forward. Nevertheless, the Library's Whittall Fund managed to accumulate a modest reserve, which sufficed in April 1970 to bring eight foreign poets from as many countries, to meet with their American translators for a series of readings and a discussion of the problems peculiar to the translation of poetry. Thus limited in numbers and scope, as well as professionally "low-keyed," the festival may have seemed more like a workshop, and indeed a profitable one, as indicated by the proceedings published in the Library of Congress brochure, *The Translation of Poetry* (1972). Perhaps Shuntaro Tanikawa best expressed the consensus in a letter afterward to the Consultant in Poetry, freely translated as, "I sensed that man was really seeking only one poem from the depths of diverse cultures."

More recently, another gathering of some literary consequence was sponsored under the auspices of the Whittall Fund on January 29 and 30, 1973— the Library of Congress Conference on the Teaching of Creative Writing. Satirically described by a participant as "the largest gathering of literary woodbees and hasbins in the history of literature," the conference was attended by several hundred writer-teachers from colleges and universities which have accredited the writing of poetry and fiction in the established curriculum. Guidance, if not leadership, of the conference, was provided by directors (some of them emeritus) of the seminars, workshops, programs, and conferences, which their respective institutions had more or less pioneered as graduate schools for creative writing rather than research: Elliott Coleman of Johns Hopkins, Paul Engle of Iowa, and Wallace Stegner of Stanford, together with John Ciardi, long director of the Breadloaf summer conference at Middlebury, Vermont.

This epochal literary gathering demonstrated a number of things about teachers and writers, and perhaps about readers also. Creating and criticizing go hand in glove, with few writers reluctant to criticize another's work. General consensus holds writing to be a craft, perhaps sometimes an art, that must be learned, but is seldom if ever taught. "Taste" is every writer's criterion, but an ambiguous esthetic-ethical gorgon nonetheless, which fixes each individual writer's vision in a particular view. But above all the conference demonstrated how completely academia has extended its establishment to encompass not merely the study of our literary past but also the creation of our literary present. Few institutions of higher learning get along without at least a writer-in-residence, and some have poet-in-residence, novelist-in-residence, and dramatist-in-residence all at once. A few support an entire corps of writers engaged in workshops, seminars, or programs producing the literature to which the local and national prizes and awards are meted out annually, frequently at the decision of juries of writers produced by those same institutions, who have established their reputations as creators, if not as judges, of literature. Indeed, it would seem that the practice of literature, like those of law and medicine, has of late passed from the status of art to the status of profession, with its own professional organization, The Associated Writing Programs.

Thus, through its Huntington Fund and Whittall Fund, the Library of Congress had been able over the years to establish a literary forum of sorts in the nation's capital. It has been able to observe with obeisance and éclat numerous literary anniversaries, the Shakespeare quadricentennial and the Dante septicentennial among others. It has been able to maintain the post of Consultant in Poetry with sufficient aplomb to contribute to the popular misconception, frequently but futilely corrected, that it is the poetlaureateship of the United States. It has, through the annual Whittall series of readings and lectures (which are the principal activity carried on by its Poetry Office) established a literary center for the nation's capital. The results of these activities have not been limited to Washington, however, as through publication of the annual lectures, and broadcasts of the readings and performances, the public at large has come to identify the Library of Congress with our national literature in something more than a library's traditional function as a repository of books. Other institutions may be mere mausoleums of culture, but here "the implacable life of silent words" resurrects continuously.

Developments in technology have enabled the Library to begin recording not only the voice but the image of the poet on TV tape. A few of the Whittall Programs have also been televised experimentally in the Library's Coolidge Auditorium and telecast in cooperation with Washington Channel 26/WETA. Perhaps more effective have been the programs worked out specifically for the television audience at the WETA studio, as for example a program recorded by poets Robert Hayden and Derek Walcott at the time of their joint reading, November 21, 1968, first telecast by WETA on September 16, 1969. Expense makes the future of such telecasts uncertain, but for archival preservation of both voice and image, TV tape has joined audio tape as an essential permanent record. And as long as the National Public Radio network continues to broadcast poetry programs presented by the Library of Congress, it is expected that the Whittall Fund will enable interested stations to receive them.

But the problem of governmental sponsorship of the arts and recognition of the artist, first tackled in the area of belles lettres by the Librarian of Congress in 1937, remains largely unsolved in both esthetic and political complexities. The establishment of the National Endowment for the Arts, as well as the Kennedy Center, both enfiladed from continuous ambush by bushwhacking critics of the right, center, and left, demonstrates that the esthetic confusions of today are no less evident than, not to say further confused with, the political ones.

The report of the National Endowment for the Arts, *The First Five Years, Fiscal 1966 through Fiscal 1970,* suggests in its summary of "Literature Programs" how pussyfooting through the political briar patch must avoid making individual awards to poets who indulge in controversial politics, whatever their merits may be as poets. Even though the report fails to list the names of those "29 exceptionally gifted but unrecognized writers" who received "Discovery Awards" in 1968—except for the half dozen who were surely discovered by nearly everybody before the National Foundation woke up (e.g., Robert Hayden and John Hawkes)—one must record the fact that the total list, if printed, would *not* have included a single poet who had obviously snapped at the hand that was feeding him. This fact stands out even more from the list of 45 presumably already discovered writers who received among them a total of $362,500 to "enable them to complete works-in-progress." There is not a Robert Bly, Galway Kinnell, or Lawrence Ferlinghetti among them. One wonders how many, if any, grants were made, and turned down, by such as these.

The Report as a whole suggests that the Foundation, wisely perhaps, is spreading governmental largess on the basis of geographic no less than esthetic criteria, and the "Literature Programs" cannot be said to suffer particularly because of this overall tendency. But only the "Literature Programs," as reported, seem to reflect obvious political criteria, though it is not partisan politics that shows through, so much as plain establishmentarianism. And, someone may ask, why not?

The spectacle of President Johnson's "Festival of the Arts" in 1965, so clumsily "managed" and controversially "recorded" for posterity by White House historian-in-residence Eric Goldman (*The Tragedy of Lyndon Johnson*, 1969), suggests that the celebration of the arts and the artist may never be quite possible with dignity in the capital of the United States of America. Only in an African republic, perhaps, can the poet chant great humanistic themes, in magnificent language, from a governmental rostrum, as the black American Poet Laureate of Liberia, M. B. Tolson, so powerfully demonstrated in his *Libretto for the Republic of Liberia*. Can anyone imagine Allen Tate, or Allen Ginsberg, in a comparable role on a Washington rostrum?

As administrator in charge of literary activities at the Library of Congress for more than twenty years, one attempted to maintain that poetry and polemics are not the same thing, although some poets have certainly succeeded in writing polemic poetry of a high order. Also, an effort was made to persuade an occasional poet that his primary function as poet was not necessarily limited to his political function as a citizen of the U.S.A. Alas, however, it was not only Eartha Kitt, who took an invitation to the White House as the best opportunity for the citizen artist to let "Government," personified in a gracious hostess, know that the hostess is really a mere hired servant of the people, in particular "yours truly."

In recent years, invitations to poets to read or lecture at the Library of Congress, under the auspices of the Whittall Fund, have more and more frequently produced problems that might have seemed impossible, or at least improbable, a decade earlier. For example, a poet noted for her feminine touch, if not tact, replied to an invitation that if she accepted, it would have to be with the understanding that before reading her poems on the stage of the Library's Coolidge Auditorium she would be obliged to denounce the President of the United States. Obviously, under that threat, it was necessary to withdraw the invitation, for the Library of Congress seemed hardly the most appropriate rostrum for that purpose.

When some months later another poet replied in a somewhat similar but less belligerent vein, an effort was made to draw a line of distinction that might possibly clarify the Library's function as an institution with a role to play in the recognition of literature. The one condition that the poet finally wished to place on his acceptance was that he must announce his intention to donate his honorarium for the reading to "Resist," which organized resistance to the draft.

Perhaps the effort to draw a line of distinction through this poetic dilemma may permit quotation of part of the "bureaucratic" reply:

> I am glad you are coming this fall. What use you make of the honorarium is, of course, your own affair, and I am sure there are many good causes which could use the money. I understand your feelings, and although I could hope that by next November some of the matters of which you disapprove, as do I and many others, might be disposed of, the likelihood seems extremely remote. There is one thing, however, that I think we all can be glad of: Our government is not monolithic. The Whittall Fund is not even taxpayers' money, but a gift fund dedicated to the appreciation of poetry! To assume that acceptance at any one time of our invitation to read poetry gives even tacit approval to the policies pursued by the political administration of that moment seems to me

to imply a belief in guilt by association which is almost as incredible, to me at least, as that assumed by the worst of the witch-hunters of another era. Worse than that, however, it seems to me to assume that good intentions of a rather remarkable woman, Gertrude Clarke Whittall, can be vitiated in perpetuity by the acts and policies of persons who may not even recognize poetry or know of the existence of the Library's poetry readings. That would be going even farther than Calvinistic dogma in assumption of a universal taint . . . . The Library of Congress provides a rostrum for poetry, not for political speeches, and when Langston Hughes read from his *Ask Your Mama,* as well as other politically charged poems, few if any felt that it was inapropos, *for it was poetry,* without doubt. Even Archie MacLeish read some pretty highly charged verse in the Coolidge Auditorium not many years ago, but I am sure he would never use an invitation to read poetry as an opportunity to make a political speech in the Library of Congress, for he knows that the Library of Congress never invites political speakers, however eminent they may be.

As it turned out, the poet did announce to the audience that he would donate his honorarium to "Resist." Moreover he read from a poem dealing with his feelings about the moral and political milieu which spoke most virulently of the government of the United States and the President thereof. There were those present in the audience who felt that at least the aspersions on the President might well have been omitted, but the roof did not cave in, and, perhaps fortunately, so little attention is paid by Congressmen or Senators to the poetry read in "their" Library* that no accounting was required of those responsible for administering the poetry readings.

In this cultural climate, poets began to avoid even the appearance of evil associations. One letter replying to an invitation to read went as follows: ". . . I naturally would feel honored to do it. However, since it *is* the Library of Congress, and since that Congress continues to appropriate funds for the conduct of the Vietnam war, I have to refuse your lovely invitation. I won't par-

---

* The Library of Congress was characterized on the floor of the House, June 4, 1971, according to the *Congressional Record,* by Representative George Herman Mahon of Texas, as merely "the creature of the Congress."

ticipate in any official government program so long as that government continues such wars . . . ." Not even one's attempted distinction between poetry and politics can suffice in such a case. One can only respect the poet's feelings about his government, particularly when, though for somewhat different reasons, they prevented the first black poet invited to serve as the Library's Consultant in Poetry, from accepting the post. The feelings of blacks about the Washington establishment is perhaps such that any black poet who accepted the post would have to risk the charge of "Uncle Tomism." Such a charge was in fact leveled at a black poet reading at the Library of Congress, by a black member of the audience. And yet it must have been less than easy to decline an appointment which might have closed with dignity the hiatus since Paul Laurence Dunbar served books at the Library of Congress as a deck attendant, long before there was a Consultant in Poetry. It is not difficult to appreciate the ambivalent feelings of any poet invited either to read his poems publicly at the Library of Congress, or to serve the Library as its Consultant in Poetry, in an era when cancellation of a performance of Lincoln's Second Inaugural Address, commissioned for President Nixon's second inauguration in a musical setting by an outstanding modern composer, was considered necessary because "the text of the work might embarrass President Nixon." (*New York Times*, January 14, 1973)

The affair of the Muse and the government at large, as well as the Library of Congress, which may have seemed a mere flirtation to some more than thirty years ago, and later a somewhat tempestuous and ill-fated liaison, has settled into an acknowledged but dubious relationship. Like all middle-aged continuations of romance, the affair may seem obviously humdrum or bitterly disillusioning. Certainly not all the announced hopes and expectations of librarians Putnam and MacLeish have been achieved, but though librarians fade and pass, the Muse stays young, and who knows what may happen?

YANKEE VERGIL — ROBERT FROST IN WASHINGTON

It makes the prophet in us all presage
The glory of a next Augustan age. . . .
A golden age of poetry and power
Of which this noonday's the beginning hour.

"Dedication: For John F. Kennedy His Inauguration"*

I

The occasion which ultimately led Robert Frost to his role as prophet was an informal reception in the Whittall Pavilion of the Library of Congress, following his talk and reading in the Library's Coolidge Auditorium on the night of October 24, 1955. As accompanying éclat to the poet's performance, the Library had mounted an exhibit of Frostiana, which included a significant selection of pictures illustrating Frost's New England and

---

* The lines from Robert Frost's poems are quoted by permission of the publisher, Holt, Rinehart and Winston. Quotations from letters and press conferences in this article are from Library of Congress files.

many photographs of the poet himself, taken over the years. He was highly pleased, not only with the exhibit but also with the audience and the reception, attended by a number of Washington's prominent figures, including such old friends as Associate Justice of the Supreme Court Felix Frankfurter and Special Assistant to President Eisenhower, Sherman Adams.

What Frost inscribed for me in a copy of his *Complete Poems* that night was: "To Roy Basler / my friend in the / seats of the mighty."

My pleasure in this inscription was not simply that of an admirer of Frost's poetry from college days more than forty years earlier. The privilege of having arranged for an affair which had been so eminently a success added special pleasure to the sense of friendship established immediately upon my first confrontation with the poet on the preceding Sunday afternoon. One meets poets and poets. Sometimes at the first meeting we hit it off, and sometimes we don't. There was a small but tricky private matter about which we understood each other, without having to apologize or explain, that lay at the root of our rapport and beginning of a friendship that would last till Frost's death.

But I was puzzled that night as I looked at the inscription again, after the occasion had been folded and put to bed along with distinguished visitor, by the suspicion that Frost might not merely be pulling my leg a bit. In the course of the two days, he had said several little things that could be indicative of something.

I was under no illusions about my proximity to "the seats of the mighty," although I *had* had my picture taken with President Eisenhower once in the White House, when presenting him with a set of *The Collected Works of Abraham Lincoln.* Furthermore, among the distinguished guests at the reception were friends and acqaintances of long standing who actually occupied positions, to use Frost's phrase, "very close to the top." Of one thing I was certain—Frost relished the Washington scene and genuinely enjoyed the attention we had given him. There was a possibility, which I would think about for two years. Could it be that Frost was interested in becoming the Consultant in Poetry at the Library of Congress? At the moment, the idea seemed a bit unlikely, but two years later there could be no doubt whatever that he had in view the "Chair of Poetry in English."

Thus, in the spring of 1958, Robert Frost became Consultant in Poetry at the Library of Congress — with a purpose. For many years his poetry had received wide acclaim indeed, but it became increasingly evident that he wanted more, and meant to get it. It was my privilege, in a small way, to aid and abet his intent. The role which he conceived for his remaining years— prophet and wiseman to the nation—he developed craftily as the stage widened, and with some luck, good timing, and a fair portion of ham acting, he was able to play out his part, perhaps farther downstage than he had ever suspected possible.

He came to discuss the terms of his appointment with the Librarian of Congress L. Quincy Mumford on May 1, and on May 12 his appointment was announced. Interest generated in the press exceeded expectations, and arrangements were made for a press conference on May 21, to be followed by a gala reception. At the press conference, Frost was in good form. After a brief reference to his pleasure in being appointed to follow Randall Jarrell, whom he described felicitously and tartly as "one of the most *pronounced* literary figures in America," reporters from the national wire services, as well as the Washington, New York, and Philadelphia (but oddly not Boston) papers, CBS, the U.S. Information Agency, and Telenews, among others, plied him with questions.

Would he continue "Jarrell's policies"? He would if he "knew what they were."

What did his position consist of? "Making the politicians and statesmen more aware of their responsibility to the arts. . . And I wouldn't have much confidence in myself that way if I hadn't been so successful in Washington lately in a law case. [Ezra Pound's release had been cleared on April 18.] But, I surprised myself. I wish—Kipling has a poem that begins 'I wish my mother could see me now.' "

How did he intend to make politicians and statesmen aware of the arts? "I guess we'll have to ask them to dinner once in a while. And then, you know, you can keep giving them your books. . . I've got one with me for somebody very high up right now—very, very high up—about as high as you can get." What would he inscribe in it? "I hadn't got as far as that, but it'll be as farmer to farmer. . . ."

Did he discuss the Pound case with the President? "No. . .the Attorney General. . .It started with Mr. Brownell, but Mr. Rogers got promoted the day after I saw him as Assistant. See, I got him promoted. . . ."

Within a few minutes, the scope of the Consultantship in Poetry at the Library of Congress had expanded beyond anything heretofore contemplated, by anyone other than Frost, at least. The questions, answers, and badinage continued for an hour, covering the Pound case as well as the only other time Frost had anything to do with the law — "for punching somebody once years and years ago."

Why? "That's too delicate a matter. I can't go into that."

President Eisenhower's fondness for a painting by Anders Zorn, Theodore Roosevelt's appointment of Edwin Arlington Robinson to a job in the New York Customs House, and Coolidge's acquaintance with the poet Dennis McCarthy, who wrote for the Boston *Post,* came in for comment.

Dwight Morrow had tried to get President Coolidge to invite Frost to the White House, and all Coolidge had replied was: "There used to be a poet by the name of Dennis McCarthy hanging around the State House in Boston."

It was Frost's opinion that we should "do something about this, bringing poets and presidents and things together. Wouldn't it be terrible if this country went down in history, like Carthage, without anybody to praise it. . .?"

As the conference went on, covering such divergent topics as socialism, the need for more study of the humanities as opposed to science, and the need for political leaders, as a reporter phrased it "to have religious faith," everyone participating had a most enjoyable time, but Frost obviously the most enjoyable of all. He was being consulted!

The reception that followed the press conference was lavish by Library of Congress standards, since Frost's publishers, Henry Holt and Company, Inc., were co-hosts. Many distinguished Washingtonians were invited and most of them came, but, in view of later developments, it is interesting to note that neither of the Senators from Massachusetts was on Frost's guest list, although the New Hampshire and Vermont delegations were invited, and came.

The news stories concerning Frost's appointment elicited general praise and approval, but lest it be thought that any poet, no matter how distinguished or venerable, can be appointed to this quasi-public office without becoming the subject of attack, a letter signed "Veteran," published in *The Washington Daily News* on June 4, protested:

> Personally, I never could understand why the taxpayer had to hire a consultant in poetry, since most taxpayers' interest in versification seldom goes beyond Edgar Guest or Ogden Nash.
>
> As a veteran of W.W. II, it's disappointing to me that Mr. Frost was appointed. How can a man, who brags about his campaign to get Ezra Pound out of St. Elizabeth's, be "cleared" for a position with the Library of Congress?
>
> Not so long ago, a better poet, and a better patriot was turned down for the job because this poet, author and esteemed medico, Dr. William Carlos Williams, was considered too democratic!
>
> Now, the Library of Congress bends over backward to employ a friend and defender of a man charged with treasonable broadcasts for an enemy during wartime. Librarian L. Quincy Mumford has not convinced me Mr. Frost merits Federal employment — either as a poet, or as a friend of Ezra Pound.

"Veteran" was mistaken, as are most critics of the Consultantship, in assuming that the taxpayer's money pays the consultant's honorarium, when in fact a modest endowment, given to the Library of Congress by the late Archer M. Huntington, provides the means for this unique post.

II

During the summer months, preparations were made for Frost's assumption of his official duties in October. Requests for appointments, as well as letters enclosing manuscripts for the consultant to criticize and asking all kinds of advice, became so numerous that it was necessary to devise form replies explaining why the consultant could not personally reply to all. But when Frost arrived on October 12 to spend his first week in residence, both his office schedule and his social schedule were full. He was consulted officially by State and Army, as well as by professors, students, and poets. He read his poems in the Library's Coolidge Auditorium to an invited audience of high school honor students and their teachers, and again held a press conference, this time sparsely attended. When told that President Eisenhower had called a press conference at the same time, he remarked, "First things first. . . I'll have to say something to him about that when I see him." When introduced to the reporters by the Deputy Librarian of Congress with an explanation that the conference had been called because the consultant's crowded schedule could not accommodate all the requests for individual interviews, he protested with good humor, "Now *you* decided all this. I ought not to be called poetry consultant. I ought to be called poet-in-waiting." He remarked that "one reason I'm here is my ambition. . . to get out of the small potatoes class." He wanted "somebody in the Cabinet for the arts. . . just to have the state recognize the existence of the arts."

This conference rambled over American poetry, with pungent comment on Pound's *Cantos,* as well as American painting, especially Frost's liking for the work of Winslow Homer, Andrew Wyeth, Thomas Eakins, and James Chapin. He had a painting by each in mind that he thought would suitably decorate the walls of the consultant's office. But he wouldn't want to have too sumptuous working conditions. "If I had a beautiful studio, I'd never paint. I'd have ladies visiting."

In reply to a question whether the world did not operate too much on the basis of "You know me, Al," he agreed. "The whole human race is. . . . How else could it be? Would I approve somebody I knew nothing about?" This reminded him of the story of a man who supported a friend for appointment to the Pennsylvania Supreme Court and was told "I don't know him. I know you. How about you taking the job?" As events were to develop for Frost, this comment had more point than anyone could then have surmised.

If his schedule did not keep him busy enough in October, it can be said that it kept several members of the Library staff more than busy enough, but to the delight of all. When he returned for his tour of duty in December, an equally hectic schedule was observed, with a public lecture and reading, "The Great Misgiving," interviews, conferences, luncheons, dinners, and by Frost's request, another press conference.

As reported in the newspapers with the headline "Frost Complains of Lack of Work," he began, "I summoned you." He wondered if he had not come to Washington on a misapprehension, to be consulted not only about poetry but about politics, religion, science—anything. "But I've been consulted only three times by the White House, only once by the Supreme Court, and not at all by Congress. I think something ought to be done about it."

What did the Supreme Court want to know? Something he had once said to the late Justice Cardozo: "The Supreme Court will bear watching because it might lose the distinction between being a referee and being a handicapper." The obvious relevance to the integration question was not lost as Frost went on, "I think the legislative department has been delinquent. The legislative department should have been tending to what the Supreme Court in desperation had to do."

He confessed that he would like to be a senator. "I wish some good senator would resign about six months before the end of this term and let me finish it out." But that was Truman's idea, too. "Then he stole it from me." His first bill to be introduced would be "to give this office of mine a real standing in the government."

He admitted to being an expert on education. "I have long thought our high schools should be improved. . . . A lot of people are being scared by the Russian Sputnik into wanting to harden up our education or speed it up. I am interested in toning it up at the high school level. . . . I would rather perish as Athens than prevail as Sparta. The tone is Athens. The tone is freedom to the point of destruction. Democracy means all the risks taken, conflict of opinion, conflict of personality, eccentricity."

Did he feel the present Administration sympathetic to the arts? It was "much more so before a recent sad event." Sherman Adams had departed from the White House. About his old friend he said, "He really cares about the arts."

His December week in Washington was made notable by the negotiation for presentation to the Library of Congress, at Frost's request, by his friend and long-time correspondent Louis Untermeyer, of several hundred letters (since edited by Untermeyer and published by Holt), which are in effect a large slice of Frost's autobiography. The promised gift was appropriately but quietly celebrated at a luncheon in honor of the two poets, but the actual deposit of the letters was not to take place for some months and would not be announced until two years later, on December 11, 1960.

Frost's complaint that Congress had not taken sufficient note of his presence had borne fruit when he returned to the Library for his week at the end of March. A Senate Resolution, sponsored by 62 senators, extended birthday greetings on his 85th anniversary. The language of the Resolution reminded him that the Senate had in a similar Resolution extended greetings on the occasion of his 75th birthday, and apologized that "although compelled by the necessities of our time to concentrate its attention on things material, nevertheless [the Senate] is fully cognizant of the value and importance to our citizens as long as our Nation shall endure of things of the spirit contained in our national literature, art, and culture."

His birthday was celebrated with fanfare, not in Washington, but in New York, where his publishers arranged a dinner to which were invited the distinguished literary lights of the nation and not a few political figures, many of whom were unable, because of public business, to attend. Among those who sent their regrets along with birthday greetings was Senator John F. Kennedy of Massachusetts.

Frost had formed a high opinion of Kennedy and believed he was a man to watch. In our occasional discussions of men in politics during the next few months, Frost was on the whole

most perceptive. He had his prejudices, but he was singularly
free of the all too common intellectual contempt for
politicians—especially politicians who fail to see things in the intellectual vogue of the moment. He could even make allowances
for some of the practical political facts which inhibited the
public expressions and acts of certain Southern politicians
whom he held in considerable respect. When I once teased him,
however, about Kennedy's rather aloof record during the
McCarthy outrage, he would not defend this failure to take a
stand, as he would defend certain Southern senators whose con-
stituencies would not permit them to espouse the Supreme
Court's decision, in *Brown et al.* He merely shrugged off the
challenge.

At the press conference held in the New York offices of his
publishers on the morning of his birthday, March 26, Frost
quickly and deliberately got into politics: "Somebody said to me
that New England's in decay. But I said the next President is going to be from Boston." When pressed to name the man, he
replied, "Can't you figure it out? It's a Puritan named Kennedy."

Although the poet's other comments made interesting news, it
was this that made the headlines across the country, as well as
in New York.

Frost's week at the Library began on March 30. It included his
usual public lecture and reading at the Library as well as one at
the Folger Shakespeare Library; a seminar for graduate students
from the local universities held in the Wilson Room of the Li-
brary of Congress; several luncheons, one at the Federal Trade
Commission, and one in the Whittall Pavilion of the Library of
Congress, attended by President Eisenhower's Special Assistant
Frederick Fox, Senator Thomas C. Hennings of Missouri and
Representative Frank E. Smith of Mississippi, among others.
But not Senator Kennedy.

A few days after Frost's departure for Cambridge, however, a
letter arrived in the Library's Poetry Office,

United States Senate
Washington, D.C.
April 11, 1959

Mr. Robert Frost
Poetry Consultant
Library of Congress
Washington, D.C.

Dear Mr. Frost:

I just want to send you a note to let you know how gratifying it was to be remembered by you on the occasion of your 85th birthday. I only regret that the intrusion of my name, probably in ways which you did not entirely intend, took away some of the attention from the man who really deserved it — Robert Frost. I want to send you my own very warmest greetings on which [*sic*] is for all of your admirers a milestone, but for you is only another day in the life of a young man.

I do, however, share entirely your view that the New England heritage is not a fading page but that it has continuing vitality and a distinctive future. I was more impressed than ever by this during the past fall when for the first time in six years I had an opportunity to move intensively across the state from town to town and to see again first-hand the very special qualities of the New England mind and New England heritage.

With best thanks and all good wishes to you,

Sincerely,

John F. Kennedy

Frost's final week as Consultant in Poetry at the Library of Congress began on May 18, with a talk and reading that night to which only members of the Library staff and their families were invited. The limited seating capacity (c. 500) of the Library's Coolidge Auditorium had been inadequate for every public reading Frost had given, and it was felt that on this concluding performance the staff, many of whom had not been able to hear him at all, should be given priority. The auditorium was filled to overflowing again, and Frost received an ovation, to which by this time he was, of course, far from unaccustomed. The usual heavy schedule of interviews, conferences, luncheons, and dinners obtained, and a reception was held in the Library's Whittall Pavilion on May 20, recorded in my diary with considerable understatement, as "a pleasant social affair which very fittingly wound up his stay at the Library in so far as the public relations aspect is concerned."

For Frost, this reception achieved the recognition of his consultantship by the largest turnout of dignitaries and wives yet seen—Ambassadors, White House officials, Supreme Court Justices, Representatives and Senators—among the latter John F. Kennedy, who almost "slipped" in, and out, after the briefest of handshakes, so that few in the crowded Pavilion besides Frost would remember, later on, just when it was the two men first met.

In view of later developments, an extremely important event took place on the night of May 19 when Frost accepted the invitation of Representative and Mrs. Stewart L. Udall to dine at their home. Frost appreciated this invitation highly, and it marked the beginning of a friendship which he renewed whenever he came to Washington. As he had observed concerning the principle of "You know me, Al," how else could it be that a poet should get selected for special recognition?

On Frost's last night, May 23, a group of the Library's staff who had worked most closely with him gave him a dinner at the Hay-Adams. It was an occasion for congratulations all around the table, not the least sincere of which were Frost's own. He was especially pleased when the Librarian invited him to continue in the capacity of "honorary consultant." Four days later, with the approval of the Librarian of Congress, I wrote Robert proposing that he serve the Library in the capacity of "Honorary Consultant in the Humanities." His reply was "Won't it be capital for us all to get together next year." And so it was. His new appointment was not announced, however, until August 27, 1959, in order not to detract from the publicity given the appointment of his successor as Consultant in Poetry, the distinguished poet Richard Eberhart, who would, in his own way, make a place for himself on the Washington scene.

III

It was agreed that the first week in May 1960 would be the most suitable for Frost's initial visit as honorary consultant, and preparations were made accordingly for a talk and reading on the night of May 2, preceded by a luncheon in his honor in the Whittall Pavilion and a press conference as usual. His own party for friends would be on the next day, and, on the night of May 4, a special talk and reading for Members of Congress, Senators, and their families would be held. On May 5, he would testify before the Senate Labor and Public Welfare Committee on Senator Francis Case's bill to establish a National Academy of Culture. His interest in another piece of legislation would not require testimony: On April 28 Senator Saltonstall had introduced for himself, Senator Aiken, and Senator Prouty S. 3439, a bill authorizing President Eisenhower to award Frost a gold medal in recognition of his poetry.

For his talk and reading on the night of May 2, he wanted the printed program to carry a special device—"The Pasture Spring" in facsimile. For this he copied the poem in very clear hand and scribbled a note to accompany it. The title, as well as the poem itself, he wrote down from memory, which accounts for the fact that the title of the little poem appears in his *Complete Poems* as simply "The Pasture." Here is his note:

April 12

Dear Roy:

The idea was to make the program something to read besides titles. You are so generous about complying with suggestions. But disregard the above if it comes too late. Just have it in print like the other quotations. I'm looking forward to renewals. And I'm not afraid of the reporters unless they stay away and accuse me of things I don't think. I'm ready for them on segregation, Romanism and Russia.

I'm here where we last saw each other in Amherst.

Robert

All in all, things appeared to be picking up just where they had left off a year before, for a week of Frost as usual. As things turned out, however, there was one near fiasco and one unprecedented but quirky stroke of good luck, along with the usual round of excitement which accompanied his visits. The near fiasco was brought about by protracted debate in the House of Representatives, with numerous quorum calls, on the Area Redevelopment Act. That this should have occurred on the night of May 4, set aside for Frost's specially prepared talk and reading for Members of Congress and Senators, was most lamentable.

Although responses to invitations had brought sufficient requests for tickets to fill the auditorium, when Frost took the stage he faced only a scattered few wives and families. Some wives were still waiting outside for their husbands. As Frost proceeded, obviously a bit miffed, he warmed to his task and gave a very fine performance, and as he talked and read, a few more wives and substitute friends and relatives began drifting in. By the time he had concluded and everyone had repaired to the Pavilion for the reception that was to follow, there were perhaps a hundred and fifty present, among them half a dozen Senators and Members who ducked in to apologize and explain the dire necessities of legislation, and then duck out.

The theme of his remarks, chosen for the historic occasion, was "anxiety," the anxiety of nations, with special reference to the U.S. vs. Russia, Israel vs. the Arab nations, etc., paralleled with allusions to history, Athens vs. Persia, Rome vs. Carthage, England vs. the Continent: "I suppose this has been going on a long time, and I suppose that is what lies ahead of us—the championship." But he cut it short, after some wandering, and began to "say" his poems. For those who came, if not for him, the evening was a success.

The luncheon on May 2 was another matter—something no one who was present will be likely to forget.

Carl Sandburg was in town to receive on the same evening a silver laurel wreath from the U.S. Chamber of Commerce—its "Great Living Americans Award." Carl's long and friendly "official" association with the Library of Congress dated from 1944, with his appointment by then Librarian Archibald MacLeish as a Fellow in American Letters. He customarily stopped by whenever in the city, to visit and chat with me, or David Mearns, Chief of the Library's Manuscript Division, or both. I had enjoyed Carl's friendship and personal encouragement as a student of Lincoln, dating from the early 1930's. At the very time in 1958 when I had been negotiating with Frost to become Consultant in Poetry, I had also signed Carl up to deliver an address on Abraham Lincoln in the Library's Coolidge Auditorium on the night of February 12, 1959. I had taken this precaution so far in advance, because Carl would be in great demand in the Lincoln sesquicentennial year. As things turned out, this was most fortunate, for this commitment to the Library was ultimately expanded by an invitation to address a joint session of the Congress at noon on the same day. Both his address before Congress and his talk that night at the Library were moving and memorable performances, but it was the former, of course, which captured the headlines from all other Lincoln Day observances, partisan or otherwise.

That the Lincoln Sesquicentennial should have enabled Carl's brief preemption of the poet's spotlight in the nation's capital during Frost's year as Consultant in Poetry was perhaps an inevitable accident. Even though it came during Frost's absence from the Library, it did not pass unobserved by Frost, as I learned when he returned for his week in residence at the end of March.

I had presented Frost a copy of a small volume of Lincoln pieces, one of them my own, which emanated from the University of Illinois' observance of the Sesquicentennial. He apparently read them that night, for the next evening he discussed them, and Lincoln generally for the first time with me. He brought up Sandburg's biography of Lincoln — was it really any good? I replied that it was a tremendous book, easy to find fault with, but all-in-all not only the most readable but the most useful, to the student of history, as a compendium of information. But, Frost wanted to know, wasn't it full of bad prose and bad free-verse, bathos, pretending to be history? I admitted that Sandburg was sometimes poetically uncritical of his sources, and perhaps had gone overboard in spots—for example, in his endeavor to convey the emotional impact on the nation of Lincoln's assassination—by employing some dithyrambic prose, but that this did not seem to me necessarily inappropriate to the historian's task. I was tempted to ask him if he had read the monumental work, or was merely reacting to what certain academic historians had said about it, but it was pretty obvious that Sandburg was neither Frost's favorite poet nor his favorite historian.

Nevertheless, when a year later I learned that Sandburg was in town on the day of our Frost luncheon, the opportunity to bring the two together seemed just too good to miss. After a brief greeting over the telephone, I proposed to Carl that he join us, if he were free. There was a pause, then—"Why should I come to a luncheon for Robert Frost?" I realized in the moment that Frost was a subject Carl and I had never had occasion to discuss, and I sensed that perhaps the feeling was mutual between them, no love lost on either side. I replied somewhat lamely that there was no good reason I could think of, except that I was asking him. "I'd like to get you two guys together, and I'll never have a better chance. I'll send a car for you."

After some chuckling, Carl agreed, "Okay, if you say so." I was elated at the prospect, but unprepared for its unfolding.

As Carl came into the Pavilion, a wool scarf about his neck and a black fedora on his head, he paused at the threshold. I greeted him and turned to Robert who, with his back toward us, was chatting with a semicircle that included the Librarian of Congress, Quincy Mumford.

I said, "Robert, here's Carl Sandburg come to lunch."

Frost turned, a glint in his eye, and grinned without moving or offering his hand. "Don't you know enough to take your hat off when you come in the house?"

Carl's throaty chuckle accompanied the exaggerated flourish with which he doffed his fedora. The familiar silver Sandburg forelock fell over his eye.

Frost: "Don't you ever comb your hair?"

Another Sandburg chuckle, as he reached into his coat pocket, brought out a comb and lifted the silver lock into place, where it stayed only for a moment. He proffered the comb to Frost. "You could use a comb yourself, haw, haw, haw!"

This broke the slightly awkward silence with a good laugh all around, for Frost's silver head was as tousled as usual.

Reaching deep in his trousers' pocket, Frost brought up the most snaggle-tooth comb I have ever seen, and ran it through his hair, with some difficulty but without much effect, to everyone's laughter. Then, finally, they did shake hands.

The luncheon group of about 25 persons, including members of the staff, the Consultant in Poetry Richard Eberhart, as well as two visiting poets, Oscar Williams and Hy Sobiloff, was fortunately large enough for each of the two elder statesmen of letters to have his own semicircle. When, after a brief libation and some photographing, we sat down to eat, the two were placed on either side of the Librarian, near enough to each other by all odds, but with myself and Oscar Williams seated facing them, to keep the quips flying without any absolute necessity of smashes or kills at the net. For as they broke away from their initial greeting, Frost had brushed off his well-worn witticism to humph, "I'd as soon play tennis with the net down as write free verse."

During the prandials, both pre and post, Carl maintained his good humor and refused every opportunity to thrust in reply as Frost became more and more obviously, but still not impossibly, tetchy in his sallies, not too *sotto-voce*, either. "The slob of the sunburnt west!"

Oscar Williams, seated opposite Frost, egged him on, though Frost needed no encouragement, while I, opposite Sandburg, kept Carl's attention directed, as much as possible, toward his acolytes at our half of the table. Carl was a sublime egoist, wholly indifferent to, if not wholly unaware of, the display of sparks that Frost's terrific if pettily competitive instinct was

generating. The hilarity was immense because everyone was
aware of how close we were skating to the thin ice that might
break and dunk us from exhilaration into dismay.

When the Librarian finally tapped his glass with his spoon
and made his customary announcement—that while this was a
merely social occasion, if either of our distinguished guests felt
any compulsion to speak, he was sure there were those who
would be glad to listen—Frost said, "Let Carl pay a tribute to
me. He oughta praise me, my poetry."

Everyone roared and Carl shook out his throatiest prolonged
guffaw to decline this gambit. Whereupon the Librarian adjourned
the affair, Frost repairing to the Poetry Office with Eberhart
and others for his press conference, and I taking Sandburg in
tow to return him to his hotel with my profound gratitude, and
relief.

I have heard others tell of times when Carl displayed a petty
or nasty disposition toward persons he held in small esteem
because of their pretensions or their pompous flatulence, but in
my many times with him I never saw this happen. In a necessarily competitive argument he could be as rough as his com-
petition, especially after a copious libation, but I never saw him
betray a hint of jealousy or upstaging. Robert, on the other
hand, was not only a born competitor, he was sometimes competitive when he need not have been because he really couldn't
help it.

This episode reinforced my observation that poets on display,
like children and people in general, will occasionally show their
essential natures rather than their manners and, when reproved, as
Frost was later by a person who knew how to and could do it,
they can pretend penitence they do not really feel. "Was I really
bad?" he asked, not the least bit contrite.

IV

Senator Saltonstall's bill authorizing President Eisenhower to
award Frost a gold medal was passed and became Public Law
86-747 on September 13, 1960, obviously too late for its pro-

visions to be carried out before President Eisenhower would
leave the White House, but the possibility that a President of
Frost's own choosing might do the honors was becoming more
likely day-by-day as the presidential campaign developed. When
election day provided the fulfillment of Frost's prediction,
rumors began to fly that Frost would participate in the
Inauguration in January, and on December 18 the fact was announced in the Washington *Evening Star*, with the comment
that "In a sense, Senator Kennedy will be paying off a campaign
debt too. All through the primaries he quoted from one of the
venerable New England poet's most celebrated lyrics, 'Stopping
by Woods on a Snowy Evening.' Inevitably, in Wisconsin and
West Virginia and points West, he bade farewell to his audience
with these lines:

> " 'But I have promises to keep,
> And miles to go before I sleep
> And miles to go before I sleep.' " (*Complete Poems*, 275)

To this account it should be added that Kennedy's choice for
Secretary of the Interior, Stewart L. Udall, had proposed Frost's
participation in the inaugural ceremony in the first place.

On Thursday, January 19, Frost came to the Library for the
luncheon we had arranged to honor his triumphal homecoming.
When he came into my office, after the briefest of greetings and
felicitations, he announced forthwith that he was going to see to
it that President Kennedy appointed me to a position of importance somewhere. Dumbfounded, I began to explain the facts of
my limited bureaucratic existence in plain terms, and when he
chided my political innocence from his now political eminence, I
became aware that he was talking rather too loud, and shut the
door, but not before he had impatiently and woundedly exclaimed,
"Don't shush me!"

He meant to do something for me and was obviously chagrined
that I didn't want him to. He had achieved a position of influence, and he meant to use it, for me. How does one grace-
fully resist a benefactor who is used to having his own way?
Especially when the improbable comes wrapped in the slightly

ridiculous. His acquiescence left me with the feeling that I had let him down, in being less than a true competitor, after his own heart.

When we joined the other members of the staff gathered in the Whittall Pavilion to honor our something more than poet laureate of the United States, I was glad I could merge my feelings in the general sentimentality of the occasion.

Inauguration day dawned bright and exceedingly cold, with the national capital muffled in the heaviest snow in several years. As I looked out the window at my sugarloaf Chevy, I yawned, "That's that!" I was devoted to Robert Frost, but not that devoted! Unfortunately, my wife, a late riser, was not only devoted to Robert Frost but also as infatuated as any wife of any New Frontiersman with J.F.K. When she woke me from my second sleep, I merely turned over. I wouldn't even have gone to see Lincoln inaugurated on such a day, and anyway we could see it better on TV.

"Get up, it's ten o'clock and there's barely time!" I couldn't believe it, but I did.

Once I had shoveled out, we mushed the Chevy to the highway and as near Capitol Hill as we could get, then booted and thick as two bears in all the outer garments we could stretch over all the inner garments we could stuff under, we heeled and toed the rest of the way, with our camera and flask, to stand among the thousands and await the opening of the New Frontier.

I shan't attempt to describe what everyone, especially those who stayed snug at home before the TV, saw better than I did, for my eyes watered and blurred, not merely from the cold and the glare of sun and snow either. But I can state that the history made before the eyes of one observer carried an emotional wallop that rose from a slough of long-winded preliminary piety to a crescendo of something I had never quite experienced before. When Robert was led to the microphones, I nearly wept. When he began stumbling through the opening lines of the new poem which he had written, "For John F. Kennedy His Inauguration," but which he couldn't "say" as he customarily did, but had to read because it was so new that it was unfamiliar even to its author, my throat simply closed. When he admitted his defeat in the glare from God on high and launched his counterattack to "say" the poem *his* President had requested, "The Gift Outright," only a school girl's phrase can name it. I was thrilled nearly to death. Even the President's exceptionally fine Inaugural Address was merely denouement, preoccupied as I was with my own thoughts. Robert had made it, as he so wanted to.

Among my thoughts was the whimsical reflection, which I voiced as we trudged away to watch the parade: "I guess it was a good thing Adlai was defeated in 1952, or Carl might have been the Prairie Vergil of the " 'next Augustan age'." My wife could never have agreed to my premise, but she got the point to my conclusion. The only precedent in American history, so far as I know, for a poet's elevation to the inaugural platform was Adlai's selection of Carl to perform the ancient duty of the ruler's chosen bard, at his inauguration as Governor of Illinois in 1948. That happened to be, also for personal reasons, the only other inauguration I ever attended.

V

Although he returned to the Library in May for his tour of duty as Honorary Consultant, Robert no longer belonged primarily to us. The date for his now established annual reading was shifted to permit his prior appearance on the night of May 1 in the State Department Auditorium, under the sponsorship of the President's Cabinet, the first of a series of such Cabinet presentations of eminent literary figures. He continued to be generous in sharing his time, however, and for the next two years made the Library headquarters for his increasingly numerous visits to Washington. His honors continued to accumulate, including the introduction of a House Resolution that he "should hereafter be known as the National Poet of the United States." Plans were made for the greatest birthday dinner yet, on the night of March 26, 1962, almost prevented by his serious bout with pneumonia early in February. When Mrs. Basler and I visited him briefly later that month at his cottage in Florida he was shakily re-

cuperating, but indomitable. "I wasn't ready to die yet."
Alluding to this illness a month later, when President Kennedy
finally presented the gold medal so long in the making, he para-
phrased the concluding lines of his poem "Away!" — "I went
right up to the grave and was so dissatisfied with what I saw
that I came back." He just couldn't afford to die and miss getting
that gold medal, or his resplendent 88th birthday dinner, at
which the great and near great of his own country, ambassadors from abroad, and assorted friends whom he never forgot,
would assemble in the Pan American Union to praise and honor
him. Nor could he forego the trip to Russia and meeting with
Khrushchev during August and September, first broached in
May at a dinner with Soviet Ambassador Dobrynin in the home
of Secretary of Interior Udall (an account of this trip by F.D.
Reeve appeared in *The Atlantic*, September 1963), nor his principal role in the National Poetry Festival held at the Library of
Congress in October. If anyone present had doubts that Frost
was *the national poet*, his talk and reading on the night of October 24, in the midst of the Cuban Crisis, dispelled those doubts
in a moment.

While Frost's proposal for a Cabinet post for the Arts seems
never to have been given serious consideration, his presence on
the Washington scene from 1958 through 1962 lent considerable
impetus to the movement culminating in the establishment of
the Kennedy Center and the National Foundation on the Arts
and the Humanities; helped bring about the continuing series of
Cabinet and White House sponsored literary and performing
arts presentations in the State Department Auditorium; and the
White House receptions, dinners, awards presentations, and
festivals honoring prominent figures in the arts and humanities
which became—until the debacle of the Arts Festival in June
1965—something of an established pattern in the national
capital. Even that somewhat dessicated federal branch, the
Smithsonian Institution, began to send forth cultural blos-
soms—concerts, lectures and whatnot—in unprecedented variety,
and the Library of Congress no longer held its unwanted distinction of being a very modest literary and musical oasis in the
federal cultural desert.

Not many lobbyists have ever achieved more for whatever cause, and none, so far as I know, has ever achieved a comparable national public image in the process. It is no denigration of the cause of the arts and humanities at large, in my book at least, to recognize that Frost's ego was his primary motivation.

He would have liked to live forever, I feel sure. If pneumonia, "the old man's friend," as he had affectionately dubbed his ailment, quoting somebody or other, when I had seen him convalescing in Florida almost a year before, had not finally persuaded him to give up on January 29, 1963, I verily believe he would have done as he threatened on his famous Christmas card:

And I may return
If dissatisfied
With what I learn
From having died. (*Away!* 1958)

YOUR FRIEND THE POET—
CARL SANDBURG

I

For the period of my life during which I was engaged in editing *The Collected Works of Abraham Lincoln*, it was my fortune to operate in and from a suite of offices in the First National Bank Building of what has been known with pride, locally at least, as "Lincoln's Home Town." One day, as I entered the elevator on the way up, I was greeted by a lawyer from the adjoining office, with the news that "Your friend the poet is upstairs looking for you." For it was as a poet that Carl Sandburg was known then, and, I think, will continue to be known for a long time to come, in spite of critical opinion at present heavily to the contrary.

If everyone in Springfield, Illinois, did not recognize Carl's "phyzzog," certainly his was the most generally known face of a living poet, there as elsewhere, in the United States. From granitic sculpture in moments of concentration or anger, to magical mobility in humor or friendship, it was a face you did not forget, not for the least reason by way of the silver lock hanging just over his left eye, which Robert Frost always insisted was barbered thus by careful design. And it was first of all a poet's face, its enigma best described by the man who saw it in the looking glass and wrote about it in the poem "Chicago Poet."

I said, 'Hello, I know you.'
And I was a liar to say so. (*Complete Poems*, 1950, p. 101)

The one thing I recall best of what I felt about Sandburg's
poetry before I came to know him personally was that the man
who wrote the poems was my guy, even when I didn't exactly
like something he said. Usually, I got around to admitting that
the way he said it was a good way, or even sometimes a splendid
way, even if nobody else in the world would have said it that
way. But then I learned to love Sandburg's poetry the same way
I learned to love Keats' poetry, not by taking somebody's word
for it but by reading it and finding it out for myself, sometimes
not easily recognizing how it was being done, or why. For me, he
had one thing above all others in common with Keats, that although frequently I could not have tolerated *how it was said*
from anyone else, it was what the guy said that counted, because it was genuine.

Like Mark Twain, Sandburg is a do-it-yourself great writer
who found his first inspiration not in literature but in life. Not
that he didn't learn from others, Whitman and Li Po for instance, but like them he was bothered about what he wanted to
say enough to try to find his own way of saying it. On every
page, in nearly every poem, his communication is one to one in a
human kinship that carries over, if one is concerned about what
he has to say. Frankly, some are not concerned.

II

In the year before Sandburg's death, the professor-critic
Gorham Munson stated, "It is doubtful if anything written in
1966 will raise the drooping reputation of Sandburg." ("Poetry
1900 to the 1930's," *American Literary Scholarship 1966*, p. 196.)
Certainly nothing Munson or any of his professorial colleagues
wrote had that effect on Sandburg's reputation, for Munson
represents very well the academic establishment which has produced a formidable bibliography of critiques and explications of
nearly everything T. S. Eliot ever wrote, but which has con-

tinued to sneer at or at best patronize Sandburg's allegedly bad poetry. One can count on fingers without using any digit more than once the number of serious critical studies of Sandburg's poetry during the last twenty years.

Buried under the avalanche of honorary degrees, medals, and prizes which followed publication of his *Abraham Lincoln: The War Years* in 1939, Sandburg was assumed by the poet-critics to have found his true profession as historian. It is a matter of fact that the historian-critics were usually far more generous in bestowing critical accolades for that incontestably great work, in spite of its recognizable shortcomings, than most of the poet-critics had ever been in assessing any of his several volumes of poetry.

From the beginning Sandburg had to become accustomed to being lectured by everyone, from Amy Lowell (for his failure to know the difference between poetry and propaganda) and Conrad Aiken ("He spills in the chaff with the wheat" and fails to recognize that "ethics and art cannot be married," *Scepticisms*, 1919, p. 147) to Carl Van Doren, who avowed his genius but lamented his lack of discrimination: "To go through his books is to stumble again and again upon heaps of slag, ore never quite melted. . . . Yet here and there from these piles of slag emerge objects of a strangely authentic beauty." (*Many Minds*, 1924, p. 150) It is remarkable how the critics so often take refuge in metaphor to convey what is wrong with Sandburg's poetry.

In the year 1950, when Sandburg's *Complete Poems* appeared, the highbrow quarterlies ignored the event, with one or two exceptions to be noticed later. The *New York Times* chose a historian, Henry Commager, and the *Herald Tribune* a playwright, Robert Sherwood, to do appreciations for the common reader. In the *Saturday Review of Literature* (November 18, 1950, p. 15), poet-critic Selden Rodman wrote lukewarmly but perceptively that "on the acceptance of 'The People, Yes' (1935) Sandburg's ultimate reputation as a poet is likely to rest . . . wrapped up to a degree with the facts of democracy." One strictly "literary" periodical, *Poetry, a Magazine of Verse*, where Sandburg's "Chicago" first shouldered its presence onto the literary horizon, could scarcely have ignored the event and chose the high priest of the current rite of modern verse, William Carlos Williams, to perform the sacrificial slaughter of the sacred bull of the lyceum circuit, who had two years before been maimed if not slaughtered by savage reviews of his over-size novel *Remembrance Rock*. Perhaps Sandburg had become too much of a national figure, fraternizing with a president and assorted senators, not to mention his favorite governor of Illinois, who had chosen him as inaugural laureate in 1948, thus setting a precedent for President Kennedy in choosing Sand-burg's rival, Robert Frost, for a similar distinction in the nation's capital, a little more than a decade later.

It was inevitable for a poet like William Carlos Williams, who wrote always, as critics have pointed out, to test his own theory of poetry, and as a result more often produced a test than a poem, to conclude that Sandburg was no poet. Indeed, he was no theoretician of poetry. In Williams' view, "without a theory, as Pasteur once said, to unify it, a man's life becomes little more than an aimless series of random and repetitious gestures." (*Poetry*, September 1951, p. 345)

They had once, years ago, been generally considered friendly rivals, Sandburg and Williams, as poets who had much in com-mon, "in the American grain," to borrow the title of Williams' most interesting book. But their principal unlikeness, as Wil-liams saw it, was the knife with which he could carve up the failure whose popular fame had so outstripped his own. Wil-liams' review showed some masterly insights into Sandburg's accomplishment, but an even greater insight into Williams' own accomplishment! Everything Sandburg did as a poet was used as a spotlight to bring out the theoretically better lineaments in the features of Williams' work. "It is up to us to discover (as he couldn't) what in that free verse may be picked up and carried forward. . . . It was a magnificent conception. He documented a thousand examples of that which the pinching poets with their neat images, take E. E. Cummings for instance in comparable passages, have merely brushed upon in passing." (*Ibid.*, p. 348) But, Williams concluded, with a smart, if not quite as ac-cidental a witticism as he pretended, "It is formless as a drift of desert sand engulfing the occasional shrub or tree and as formed.

The Collected [sic] *Poems* make a dune-like mass; no matter where you dig into them it is sand. (Sandburg! I didn't think of that. It seems as if the name itself has gotten into it.)" (*Ibid.*, pp. 350-351) Crap! How naive did Williams think *Poetry*'s readers could be? Thus, as a critic, he had only metaphor at his command, even as Carl Van Doren and Conrad Aiken had had a quarter of a century earlier. All-in-all, Williams' performance was one of his most scintillating, if unreliable, commentaries on literature.

In the midst of the depression, Ben Belitt, like most poet-critics of Sandburg, when reviewing *The People, Yes*, was disturbed by what he felt to be the surplus of propaganda and the scarcity of poetry. Quoting Sandburg's line addressed to the Chinese philosopher in the poem—"Was he preaching or writing poetry or talking through his hat?"—Belitt concluded that "Sandburg has devoted the greatest part of his energies to the first, considerably less to the second, and nothing at all to the last." Such anticlimatic praise tells us chiefly that Belitt was writing for *The Nation*. (August 22, 1936, p. 212)

Sandburg's "preaching" frequently does not appeal even to the professor-critics who find his poetics to stand up under close analysis. Thus Professor Gay Allen complains in the *South Atlantic Quarterly* (Summer 1960, p. 323) that Sandburg's "delicacy, and his painting by a few deft strokes, like the Chinese or Japanese artist," as well as his "oblique approach and (paradoxically) deep etched implications," which Allen believes to be the better aspects of his poetry, "are often obscured by his banjo-strumming and preaching." It is clear that certain aspects of Sandburg's poetry repel certain readers. Some who apparently find no conflict between Eliot's preaching and poetry find Sandburg's preaching obnoxious. After all, word for word and line for line, Eliot's poetry contains a higher proportion of preaching than Sandburg's does. It is not preaching per se that turns the professors off, but what is preached. Of course, I do not agree that preaching and poetry are necessarily mutually exclusive in any case. Some of the best of Eliot, and of Sandburg, not to mention Shelley, Wordsworth, and practically every great poet, lies in the fine blend of their particular gospel and their way of getting it across, or trying to. They never succeed, of course, with readers predilected to dislike.

As his gospel does not appeal to some, his sentiments do not appeal to others. Professor Louis Rubin, reviewing *The Complete Poems* in the *Hopkins Review*, (Winter 1951, p. 63) wrote sympathetically of Sandburg's poetics, but complained, "What is bad in Sandburg is not his poetics, but his sentimentality. And when he is good, it is not because he sings of the common people, but because he has an extraordinarily fine gift of language and feeling for lyric imagery." One may agree with Rubin's principle here but question its significance. Can it be denied that some of the best of Sandburg's "fine gift of language," as of Lincoln's, was called into play by his love of common people? Common people inspired Sandburg to some of his best words, and I am afraid that some of his critics are influenced occasionally by their own contrary sentiments. The truth is that Sandburg liked so many disparate individuals that he sang of "the people" naturally, without the overtones of odd intimacy that Whitman injected into his poems to man en masse.

Now lest anyone suppose I think Sandburg perfect, there's no denying that he has his faults, particularly as historian and prose writer—"insufferable" said Edmund Wilson in *Patriotic Gore*. But it may be wondered, even as historian, by way of odious comparison, whether in a long career Sandburg ever effused so much insufferability as Wilson did in his self-indulgent *The Cold War and the Income Tax: A Protest.*

III

The looseness of Sandburg's diction, combined with the looseness of his rhythms, is alleged by nearly all his critics to defeat his effect as a poet, and his surplus of rhythm is often alleged to ruin his prose. He was not discriminating, as a poet must be. He is allegedly not Whitman's equal because he did not limit himself to Whitman's discipline (now recognized by every college professor) of "organic" rhythms, of the sea, of the breath, the incremental repetitions of the King James Bible, catalogs, or whatnot; or on the other hand, Whitman's, by comparison, rather timid experimentation with a new American poetic diction—the two aspects of Whitman which a critic can now asseverate was "the natural expression of the poet's sensibility." And of course, Sandburg fails to accomplish what either Frost or Eliot did by sticking pretty much to the iambic line. Yet, as Oscar Cargill said in the *English Journal* (April 1950, p. 177): "With a guitar to strum and a sympathetic audience, Carl Sandburg could make Harry S. Truman's budget message sound, if not like 'Lycidas,' at least like Allen Tate's 'Ode to the Confederate Dead.' " This comment recognizes one of the certain facts about Sandburg's poetry, if not Harry Truman's prose, which he made the most of as a troubadour. He was indisputably one of the two best platform poets among modern bards, because he and Frost had at least one thing in common: each had a perfect understanding of the peculiar rhythms, tonality, and color of his own poetry, and an uninhibited willingness to perform it before an audience.

Frost's rhythms are masterly within their limited scope, but Sandburg's rhythms reach far beyond the relative restrictions of Frost's, and his diction is far more various and adventurous, if not always profound, for the simple reason that his esthetic practice controlled his theory, rather than the other way around. Frost's often repeated jest—that he'd as soon play tennis with the net down as write free verse—was taken less seriously by Frost than by some of his acolytes, for he would admit that if you did play without a net, it could be one helluva different game—if you could keep up to it! He thought Sandburg didn't, of course. And yet, there is a poetic imagery and a rumble in Sandburg to be found nowhere else.

In the subway plugs and drums,
In the slow hydraulic drills, in gumbo or gravel,
Under dynamo shafts in the webs of armature spiders,
They shadow-dance and laugh at the cost. (*Complete Poems*, p. 154)

Two brief passages may illustrate the respective poet's respective art—an informal image in formal rhythms and a formal image in informal rhythms—each poetically to its purpose, making formal seem informal and informal seem formal, or vice versa, depending on whether one's eye or ear is the more sharply tuned. One suspects the critics have better eyes than ears when they find Frost more the poet in musical matters. Meter and rhythm—

> Like girls on hands and knees that throw their hair
> Before them over their heads to dry in the sun ("Birches,"
> *Complete Poems*, p. 152)

Yes — but —

> The woman named Tomorrow
> sits with a hairpin in her teeth
> and takes her time
> and does her hair the way she wants it . . . (*Complete Poems*, p.
> 183)

When the critics and professors come to appreciate Sandburg's esthetic as well as Sandburg did, they too perhaps can interpret his poetry as effectively as he did. But they will have to do this for themselves before they can interpret for others. And they will have to escape the Prufrock syndrome before they can begin. For example, Randall Jarrell, whom Frost once dubbed "one of the most *pronounced* literary figures," passed off Sandburg's poems as mere "improvisations." Jarrell admitted that "it is marvelous to hear him say *The People, Yes*, but it is not marvelous to read it as a poem." ("Fifty Years of American Poetry," *National Poetry Festival, Proceedings*, Washington, 1964, p. 129) One wonders, did Jarrell really ever try? Ernest Hemingway once made a remark to the effect that critics frequently start with something that they never establish to be true and go on with the assumption that it is. Hemingway, incidentally, held a higher opinion of Sandburg's art than Jarrell did.

The reason why Eliot's inspired doggerel "The Hollow Men" has been ranked by the literary establishment of our era as a significant poem while Sandburg's "Caboose Thoughts" has been largely ignored will remain for future literary historians to analyze, but I hazard the guess that the outcome will have as much to say in the long run for the intrinsic poetry of Sandburg's rhythms, diction, metaphor, or what-have-you, as for Eliot's. If either of these poems has flourished by reason of an adventitious and forced feeding in a hothouse intellectual climate, it is certainly not Sandburg's.

Sandburg never suffered, apparently, from the psychoemotional dyspepsia which afflicts the likes of T. S. Eliot and Allen Tate and which has appealed so largely to the academics for purposes of classroom diagnosis and learned papers. It has been the Puritan heritage of all English departments to suffer a common misery with Eliot. The misery derives from adolescent discovery that Adam and Eve were probably no myth, but, like the professor's own fathers and mothers, whom they represent psychologically, were the persons who *got there* long before them. They have been predilected to find Eliot's "reality" stimulating because it tickles their own sense of guilt and indulges them in the vicarious pleasures of psychodramatic self-immolations, where the witch-at-the-stake (or Christ-on-the-Cross?) is the poet's psyche, but the intellectual pleasure is the professor's, and by mishap also the student's, as he grows, espaliered in the proper tradition.

The pity of this tradition is that it eventuates in the Beckett-Burroughs nadir for "the best minds of our generation," and not in Eliot's hoped-for but never achieved new version of Dante's paradise.

It is obvious that Sandburg is not "high church"; he is not even "church." He is some kind of pagan mystic, without benefit, however, of deriving from the proper Hindu sources.

IV

The fact that Sandburg is a mystic is perhaps best illustrated by his repeatedly avowed belief that everything will work out.

> In the darkness with a great bundle of grief
> the people march,
>
> In the night, and overhead a shovel of stars for keeps,
> the people march:
> "Where to? What next?" (*Complete Poems*, p. 617)

How contradictory and inconsistent can one be—a former socialist who not only came to celebrate rugged individualism in his own way but made his own fortune by doing his own thing, come hell or high water! And with a mystical conviction that simply smells of common people.

Even a sympathetic and perceptive critic like Daniel Hoffman is troubled by this contradiction, or rather by his feeling that Sandburg fails because he does not—and Hoffman cannot—reconcile the disparities. Emerson's and Whitman's rational but sympathetic critics had the same difficulty. Sandburg's practical mysticism may not be as profound as Emerson's or Lincoln's, but it is certainly as pervasively poetic as Whitman's. Hoffman and Morton Zabel and others who do not sneer, although sympathetic and perceptive, are critically circumscribed by their perspective, which sees Sandburg as naturally "limited" by his "belief in common speech and popular democracy as the basis for art" to "one or another form of realism." They believe he is merely attempting "to transcribe from nature," as a sort of animated television camera. This is all the more strange from Hoffman, when he analyzes with telling effect the pattern of poetic organization which he as a poet detects in Sandburg's allegedly amorphous mass of detail. But esthetic rightness is not enough, even for Hoffman. If it does not hang together theoretically and systematically, then it doesn't work as poetry for him any more than it does for William Carlos Williams.

This notion of Sandburg's realism began with "Chicago" and "Fog," when it was conventional for commentators, critics, and professors to call Sandburg a "realist," with "imagistic" overtones. These were the two literary words of the day, by which the then "new" poetry was categorized and catalogued. That neither term fit Sandburg very well was obvious, but words must be found by critics to abstract the recalcitrance of both the fluid and the concrete.

In regard to Sandburg's realism, Allen Tate has recently said with some tartness that "Carl Sandburg, who had all sorts of 'real' jobs, got less reality into his poems than T. S. Eliot got into his." (*Cultural Affairs*, No. 4, p. 48) Tate may be right, at least to the extent of his own understanding of reality, in that the reality which Eliot got into his poems was that which Tate knew at first hand, but in which Eliot was his master. This has been obvious for years to anyone who reads both Eliot and Tate with appreciation. But one can go further than this in agreeing with Tate, to say that Sandburg's reaction to his experience of reality was essentially, in a scientific age, where the animism of the primitive poet could not be primitively adopted, that of Emerson and Whitman, and before them that of primitive poets the world over. It is an undifferentiated outlook in which things no less than words are symbols and are both "real," for purposes of art (magic), if not for science. It is this quality perhaps which prompted Mark Van Doren's comment that "he knows better than any of his contemporaries how to put a flowing world on paper." (*The Nation*, October 31, 1928, p. 457)

Even a consistent poet changes, and his milieu sometimes changes even more. Sandburg's good-humored response to Kenneth Rexroth's query—"Where is the Sandburg who talked of picket lines? Where is the Sandburg who sang of whores?"— as reported by Harry Golden, highlights the inability of his latter-day critics to keep their eyes on the ball: "I am eighty-five years old. I am not going to talk about whores at my age. As far as the union boys are concerned, they are playing the dog races in Miami."

Of course, the professors have not entirely neglected Sandburg in recent years. Daniel G. Hoffman, Oscar Cargill, Mark Van Doren, Louis Rubin, and Gay Allen, among others, have written with perception and appreciation of what they like, and Richard Crowder has produced a critical biography of considerable merit in spite of its defensive tone. The net effect, however, seems to be that the knowledgeable student of literature must at least halfway apologize for believing Sandburg to be even a genuine poet, not to say a great poet. To an extent it is the case of Whitman and Twain all over again—that it takes some years of educating the educators to an esthetic more ample than their tradition allows. But more than this—if I may be allowed my own metaphor for what is *right* with Sandburg's poetry—it is a question of appetite and taste for a prairie spring salad of succulent poke and dandelion leaves and a few green onions, seasoned with vinegar and bacon drippings, rather than the salad of sophisticated spinach, lettuce, and endive (*ahndeev*, if you please), delicately tossed in a properly unwashed bowl that preserves the aura, not merely of proper garlic, but generations of proper garlic, mildly rubbed. Does one have to recognize only one or the other of these as poetry?

> Shake back your hair, O red-headed girl.
> Let go your laughter and keep your two proud
>   freckles on your chin. (*Complete Poems*, p. 166)

or

> A woman drew her long black hair out tight
> And fiddled whisper music on those strings. ("The Waste
> Land," *Collected Poems 1909-1962*, p. 67)

Instead of trying, in the theoretically determinate and differentiated tradition of Western art in general and poetry in particular, either the brand of William Carlos Williams or that of T.

S. Eliot, to create, or re-create, a religiously, or (for Williams at least) theoretically, valid world of myth and symbol in the twentieth century, Sandburg reverted to the primary poetic task of trying to apprehend by naming. He would be particular in the things he chose and in the words he found to name them, but he would not be discriminating by anyone else's theory in his choice, and he would be thankful for his luck in finding. His esthetic was Confucian: nothing is right, proper, or ordered theoretically, but everything lies in an esthetic pattern of relationship which must be directly apprehended to be appreciated. It was also Emersonian. Remember "Beauty is its own excuse for being" and "Each and All." Sandburg's "Tentative (First Model) Definitions of Poetry" and his "Notes for a Preface" to *Complete Poems* are his naming of his own indeterminate esthetic, which permitted "the synthesis of hyacinths and biscuits," take it or leave it.

If the professors have decided for the present to "leave it," one may suspect that it is barely possible another academic generation may decide to "take it." After all, it has required the better part of a century for most professors to adopt Whitman as their own, and make of him not just a course but, in some places, a series of courses. It may well become as academically profitable to analyze Sandburg's free verse as it will be to analyze the prose poetry or poetic prose of Saint-John Perse, the only other major poet in our day who has leaned heavily on Whitman without imitating him. Among the literary ironies, not the least pyritic is that Perse received the Nobel Prize, but the distinguished Swedish-American poet did not—except at second hand by accolade of Hemingway. It is not inconceivable, I think, that *Cornhuskers* or *The People, Yes* will yet speak in the space age already upon us with more to say of reality than *The Waste Land* does. And it is more than just barely possible that even the poetic questions Sandburg asked in poem after poem are better than many poetic answers long outmoded, as in the first, and maybe the best, thing he ever wrote about Abraham Lincoln.

In a Back Alley

Remembrance for a great man is this.
The newsies are pitching pennies.
And on the copper disk is the man's face.
Dead lover of boys, what do you ask for now?[1]

Sandburg's entire oeuvre is an elaboration on the theme of a letter he wrote to his bride-to-be from Two Rivers, Wisconsin, 23 April, 1908:

Back from a long hike again—sand and shore, night and stars and this restless inland sea—Plunging white horses in a forever recoiling Pickett's charge at Gettysburg—On the left a ridge of jaggedly outlined pines, their zigzag jutting up into a steel-grey sky—under me and ahead a long brown swath of sand—to the right the ever-repelled but incessantly charging white horses and beyond an expanse of dark—but over all, sweeping platoons of unguessable stars! Stars everywhere! Blinking, shy-hiding gleams—blazing, effulgent beacons—an infinite, travelling caravanserie—going somewhere! "Hail!" I called. "Hail—do you know? do you know? You veering cotillions of world's beyond this world—you marching, imperturbable splendors—you serene, everlasting spectators—where are we going? do you know?" And the answer came back, "No, we don't know and what's more, we don't care!" And I called, "You answer well. For you are time and space—you are tomb and cradle. Forever you renew your own origin, shatter to-day and re-shape to-morrow, in a perpetual poem of transformations, knowing no goal, expecting no climax, looking forward to no end, indulging in no conception of a finale, content to move in the eternal drama on which no curtain will be rung. You answer well. I salute you to-night. I will see you again and when I do again I will salute you for you are sincere. I believe you O stars! and I know you! We have met before and met many times. We will meet again and meet many times."—All this time I

was striding along at a fast pace, to the music of the merry-men.
The merry-men, I forgot to explain, ride the white horses and it is
the merry-men who give voice to the ecstasy and anger and varying humor of the sea. The tumultuous rhythms of the merry-men
and a steady ozone-laden wind led me to walk fast and when I
turned from the sea, there burst on my vision, the garish arc-
lamps of the municipality of Two Rivers. So I turned to the sky
and said, "Good-by, sweet stars! I have had a good companion-
ship with you to-night but now I must leave star-land, and enter
the corporation limits of Two Rivers town. Remember me, O
stars! and remember Paula down in Princeton, Illinois! and if any
agitators appear in star-land, let them agitate—it will be good for
them and for all the little stars." And as I plodded down a narrow
street fast past the hovels of fishermen and the tenements of fac-
tory workers, I quoted from the bare-footed, immortal Athenian,
"The gods are on high Olympus—let them stay there." Yes, let the
gods who are on high Olympus stay where they belong. And let us
turn to the business of rearing on earth a race of gods.[2]

Thus to apprehend and to name is the essence of Sandburg,
and it stays. Though written to Lilian Paula Steichen, it speaks
to me. It says something I like to hear today just as I first liked
to hear "Caboose Thoughts," all too many years ago.

It's going to be all right—do you know?
The sun, the birds, the grass—they know.
They get along—and we'll get along. (*Complete Poems*, p. 94)

[2] From *The Letters of Carl Sandburg* edited by Herbert Mitgang, © 1968 by
Lilian Steichen Sandburg, Trustee. Reprinted by permission of Harcourt,
Brace & World, Inc.

PROTEUS AS APOLLO: THE POETRY OF MERRILL MOORE

I

Among his contemporaries, Merrill Moore has certainly not been the poet most neglected by serious criticism, although it is true that none of his later books received the attention from reviewers which was accorded to *The Noise That Time Makes* (1929), and in fact the "highbrow" poetry journals neglected to notice most of his volumes at all. His poetry has been the subject of extended essays in the quarterlies, however, by his friends Louis Untermeyer, Henry W. Wells, and Dudley Fitts, and of a book by Henry W. Wells, *Poet and Psychiatrist, Merrill Moore, M. D.* (1955). For an extended discussion of Moore's themes, subjects, predilections, and compulsions, I am happy to refer the reader to Henry Wells. Although it is likely that his will not be the last word on the blend of science and imagination, the analysis of fear, the analysis of love, or the analysis of death which is to be found in Moore's poems, I certainly could not do more sympathetic exposition in less space than accomplished in his book. I therefore will try to attend to the primary question: What kind and what quality of poetry is Moore's?

Any serious criticism of Moore tends to boggle at his poetic style, or his lack of one—his apparent indifference to cliché, flatness, and the clumsy effects into which his devotion to colloquial diction and rhythm frequently leads him. It is significant, I think, that most of his literary friends and advisers seem to like his poetry in spite of, rather than for, some of his stylistic traits, and are constantly apologetic even when expressing admiration, as for example Henry Wells: "Although the language may be less than impeccable, an intensely and deeply realized human condition emerges that shapes the poem." (p. 82) Or again, Dudley Fitts comments: "But it must be confessed that this flatness is not always a conscious device. In many instances—perhaps in a majority of instances—the bathos-line is simply the result of careless composition." ("The Sonnets of Merrill Moore," *Sewanee Review*, 1939, p. 16)

At worst, Moore appears to be an indifferent poet who cares so little for poetry that he writes badly in "a kind of rhymed and butchered prose," with a diction "for the most part very, very approximate, to speak as charitably as possible." These phrases were used by Ivor Winters (*Poetry*, 1930, p. 104) in a review of *The Noise That Time Makes*, a volume which I find in retrospect to contain, on the whole, Moore's most carefully composed poems. Certainly if Winters could write so harshly of *The Noise That Time Makes*, there are no adequate words left to describe some of the verse in Moore's *A Doctor's Book of Hours* (1955) or *The Hill of Venus* (1957), to which I shall return later.

On a more tenable middle ground stand Louis Untermeyer, Dudley Fitts, and Henry Wells. They judge Moore to be a natural poet of talent and power who has never submitted his exuberant, prolific, and experimental art to sufficient discipline. On the peak of praise, William Carlos Williams declaims enthusiastically that "Merrill Moore's sonnets are magnificient," (*Sonnets from New Directions*, Foreword). After such tribute, one may ask if it is possible that Moore, in the vernacular tradition of Whitman (and William Carlos Williams!), has done for the classical English sonnet what the Renaissance poets did in their vernaculars—remodeled the esthetic? If so, as Dr. Williams would have us believe, what is this esthetic but that *poetry is anything one chooses to put into a series of lines?* If this is Moore's esthetic, I am inclined to stand on less advanced ground.

I should admit at this point that what I have to say about Merrill Moore's poetry will probably not satisfy anyone much better than it will myself, and I knew I could not be satisfied, even when I began to write this article. The truth is that Merrill Moore's verse has, for more than a quarter of a century, so irritated and so interested me that I can place him in good company along with T. S. Eliot as one of the two poets whose work I most frequently, and sometimes simultaneously, admire and detest. This ambivalence toward Moore's work I fully recognize to arise for quite different identifiable literary reasons from those responsible for my similar reaction to Eliot. But having given myself the benefit of a certain amount of self-analysis in order to ascertain, if possible, the subconscious cause, I have determined that, to the best of my knowledge, both reactions stem from one source, my uncomfortable suspicion that both Moore and Eliot are charlatans under their skin,—as poets, that is—I should never question their respective professional integrities nor certainly their rectitude and sincerity as gentlemen. But, as father image of the Poet, for me neither of these will do—they are idols, with feet of cinder cement and plexiglass, respectively.

Surely I must get out of this mess before I proceed. But how? Shall I confess further that, to me, Moore and Eliot are, in wholly divergent ways, two of the most successful failures in modern literature because neither of them was, for example, as true a believer in poetry as Ezra Pound, whatever his faults. And further that they are merely the greatest of a host of pseudo-poets in this century who fail again and again because they do not believe in poetry, in spite of their frequent genius? Since Walt Whitman, only a few major American writers (maybe two at most) demonstrate to my satisfaction that they truly believe in poetry. Lest the reader be as hard on me as I am on others, before I go further, let me ask: regardless of what place you assign to the best or worst of Wordsworth or Tennyson, do you doubt that those worthies believed in poetry? Very well, then, one cannot doubt their belief, which is as implicit in the least as in the greatest of their works.

This I cannot say for either Moore or Eliot, or for most of their contemporaries who write poetry. Eliot's work repeatedly shows that he believes in rhetoric and occasionally that he believes in literary scholarship, but rarely in poetry. Moore's work repeatedly shows that he believes in rhetoric (albeit not Eliot's) and occasionally that he believes in science (including medicine and psychiatry to a limited extent), but seldom in poetry.

But less about Eliot and more about Moore and what his poetry is like.

II

Reading Moore's poems, *passim,* is something like reading a newspaper in verse, an Olympian sort of *Modern Times,* which is reported, edited, and published by an Ed Howe (or a John Trotwood Moore) who was born fifty years too late, was diverted into psychiatry, and who took the U.S.A. for his metropolis, right along with him into the front seat of his automobile (or Pullman berth) when he went, or into his office (or den) when he stayed, and who somehow wrote everything in units of fourteen lines, or thereabouts. To carry the analogy a bit further, the contents of this Olympian news and gossip medium is reportorial first, editorial second. In the truly liberal vanished tradition of another day, it is rarely or never guided by the money that runs the place and is doing this job "in the public interest" for the ulterior purpose of moving readers toward or away from something which is more or less (often less) clearly understood, though its attractiveness is always appreciated. Although the "news" reported is for the most part of small rather than large events, when the event is large the "editor" knows how to present it in perspective:

> Limitation is the price of value,*
> I began to discover in March, 1942

---

* All poems are quoted by permission of Mrs. Merrill Moore, who holds the copyright.

Enormous shifting of the trains at night.

"Universes are plentiful as blackberries"—
What professor of astronomy once said that?

Anyhow the thing stuck in my mind
And went from one point to its destination
Quietly and almost silently,

And no one paid attention to the noise,
But all slept, kept on sleeping as the train
Bumped and lumbered through the foggy night,

While over it and far above the fog
Orion threatened Taurus with the Dog
Across the River glittering
                                    as the sky

Wheeled and circled imperceptibly.
And the Nation slowly found itself at war. (*Illegitimate Sonnets*,
p. 15)

Again, reading Moore's poetry is like reading a sort of Parnassian *Readers' Digest*, wholly rather than partly written to order, by a remarkable stable of Heliconian hacks assembled for the purpose of getting out a Twentieth Century Issue that will preserve for all time the essence of *It*, triple distilled occasionally, but always at least once, through the editorial worm which turns sensations and ideas in rough draft into acceptable copy, not always at the recommended temperature, but refined sufficiently to provide an effective stimulant. The ingredients of the digested articles are always of "human" interest, and although they seem clearly to have been written by different hands (minds?), they have had one editor who did things (frequently not well advised) to what had already been done, as Henry Mencken once revised the articles he accepted for the *Mercury*, to make them *more so*! In the section devoted to memorable experiences, for example, we might find this:

Moment of Confusion While Traveling

He was sleeping, on a train, (it was past midnight
Snug in the belly of a Pullman car
Lower 10 Car 12 to be exact;
Poems always benefit from fact),

When suddenly he awoke but could not tell
Actually which side was left or right
And veritably which was south or north,
Even though he tried, ten seconds worth.

Perhaps it was a bump or jolt that woke him
Or some invisible danger that bespoke him;

Anyhow, he sought for orientation
And finally found it by the constellation
Cassiopeia, which he saw when he raised the curtain
Then he fell back to sleep soon, safe and certain.

Because he realized that he was traveling west,
For he remembered that old stars are best
And Cassiopeia is always in the north;
And worry is not worth one second's worth
Of loss of sleep, so diligently he
Returned to it, his own best therapy. (*A Doctor's Book of Hours*,
p. 202)

On a somewhat higher elevation, reading Moore persistently
and continuously is something like reading the *Journal* of a
twentieth century Nathaniel Henry Waldo Moore who left Nashville, Tennessee (and literature) to rusticate in Boston, chopping
clinical wood or spreading clinical manure, all the while observing, noting, meditating (quickly) and concluding (tentatively) in
entries of fourteen lines, more or less.

Here is Nathaniel jotting down an observation for keeps (not
the New England *Journal*, obviously):

Association

Do you remember after we left Ruegen
(We took the train at Stralsund for Berlin),
The second class compartments we were in?
We took the ferry to the German mainland
From Ruegen,
                    you remember the Deutsche Reichsbahn,
And how we got off the train, out of the cars
And onto the ferry, how the passengers
Were walking up and down the ferry, when the rain
Suddenly started falling on us there
While we walked in and breathed the North Star air.

Do you remember the fresh rain striking our faces,
How it felt? Cool, pelting, wet;
                              and then the places
We passed on the ferry, saw from the train window—

Where do you suppose that rain is now? (*M*, p. 80)

Here is Henry mixing some thorough mysticism with Tennessee truth:

You Do

Living life you can choose many ways,
But much depends upon the kind of days
Fate or whatever you want to call it brings
You in which to be you. Winter sings
A different song from summer, you will learn,
And summer brings sunlight, sunlight to burn
Your skin with as you labor, or to fan
Your forehead for, if you're a lazy man.

And much depends on how you happen to look,
Dark, or fair, regular, irregular,

But most especially, whether short or tall;
If you are tall, things will be easier;
If you are short you will probably have to work
Harder and in the end get more after all. (*M*, p. 40)

And Twentieth Century Waldo saying over again what he has said before, in the idiom of modern incidentalism:

Nothing can be too Damnable or Odd

Nothing can be too damnable or odd
To suit the ancient cleverness of God,

Nothing can be too petty or too vain
To please His angels singing in the rain,

Nothing is too sordid or too crude
To mock His devils hiding in the wood,

Nothing is too dangerous or crass
To tire His serpent hiding in the grass:

And so we find there is not any end
To how His powers weave, His forces blend,

And so we see there is not any knowing
The precise way His favor may be going:

There is not any start or any stop
Without Him being bottom, middle, top. (*M*, p. 66)

And finally, here is Dr. Norman Vincent Moore (a distant Twentieth Century cousin of Waldo who appears infrequently, I am happy to report):

Infinite interest is all you need
To find the soil on which to sow the seed
Of infinite interest and endless joy
At what the world affords you as a toy. (*M*, p. 69)

III

This game of authors may be played more seriously. Coleridge played it with Shakespeare and Sophocles, observing that "times and manners lend their form and pressure to genius." So Shakespeare is to Sophocles as Westminster Abbey is to the Pantheon, as diversity is to unity. Shakespeare, like Westminster Abbey, comprised in Coleridge's view "a multitude of interlaced materials great and little, magnificent and mean. . . and yet so promising of our social and individual progression that we would not, if we could, exchange it for that repose of the mind which dwells in the forms of symmetry in the acquiescent admiration of grace."

What then of Merrill Moore? Shall we say he is to Shakespeare as the Empire State Building is to Westminster Abbey? Hardly, but, and preferably, I suggest, as an up-to-date suburban shopping center is to Westminster Abbey: sensible, uniform (approximately), efficient, utilitarian, with everything available that one ever thought of and quite a few things that have been thought of for him by someone else, and withal so definitely within reach, useful, informative, and stimulating that even if it leaves us restless and dissatisfied we would not exchange it, if we could, for whatever grandeur and interlaced magnificence. But somehow I cannot say this with the entire confidence that Coleridge had about not exchanging Shakespeare for Sophocles. Why?

Without benefit of Freud, Coleridge maintained that the poet's true genius lies in his unconscious activity, where poems grow, rather than are made, as a fusion of external and internal in which "the conscious is so impressed on the unconscious as to appear in it." This creative imitation, as opposed to mere copying of nature, is perhaps what one finds all too seldom in Moore. For the most part, he writes off the top of his mind, consciously, often accurately, intelligently, and cleverly, but also often carelessly and superficially. This is not only true when he is writing of people and things observed, analyzed, and understood (appreciated), but also when he is projecting self in a symbol or

series of symbols. His ability as a psychiatrist is everywhere
suggested in such a book as *Clinical Sonnets*, but seldom does his
genius as a poet preempt his role as psychiatrist. When it does,
one has the startled feeling of a fish which has warily swum
around an assortment of limp worms and flashy lures, and grab-
bing a true minnow, finds himself deep hooked and rising willy
nilly and unexpectedly out of his watery indifference into an excruciating atmosphere which can be endured only if prosaic gills
can be traded for poetic lungs.

I am aware that this fishy analogy was in all probability
suggested to me as a perversion of Moore's sonnet "With Little
Bait," which is interestingly enough the penultimate poem "Of
Prophecy" in the book *M*.

With Little Bait

I drew marvelous fishes out of the sea,
With little bait; it must have been an art.

It was they who played the stupid part.
Leaping, flashing their white bellies at me.

Some were enormous, some were gaunt and lean,
Some with cherubic expressions on their faces;

I never knew there were so many places
Where fish abounded and not pleocene
Fish but real ones, moderns of every sort,
Catastrophe for them, for me a sport,
With little bait and very little line.

I wonder if others' experiences were like mine;
Whenever I came near water they would appear
And snap at my hook as if they had no fear. (*M*, p. 897)

Having borne witness to his prowess, I cannot object to this
bragging which he does as a metaphysical angler. But being
something of a fisherman as well as a fish, I cannot help observ-

ing, regardless of whether his fish symbolize his poetic imagery or the readers whom he catches, what a mess his tackle box is in! He is the after-work sportsman who seldom has time, in his haste to wet a line, to observe the sacred rites which are dear to the heart of the ritualist of fishing. And at all costs he will catch fish; apparently he does not care what variety so long as he is pulling them in.

Let's take an example of each kind of thing I am talking about in Moore's work: 1) the creative imitation and 2) the mere copy of things observed. The two pieces face each other in the book *M*. Both of them deal with simple observations, which seem to have overtones for the poet, and may have for the reader as well. One of them never germinated in the poetic process of the unconscious about which Coleridge speculated. One of them did germinate, and grew; how far it grew I shall leave to the reader to decide, but I hope I need not have to designate which of the two pieces I am talking about. There is no point to any discussion of what is and what is not poetry unless we are intuitively agreed about it.

The Contents of Waste Baskets

Who considers the contents of waste baskets
Of negligible or supernumerary worth?
Who, reaching into one, would bring forth
Envelopes (opened) or sheets of crumpled paper
That were the letters the envelopes contained?

House-maids? No, they think of their lovers' eyes
As they empty waste baskets. The janitor? No.
As he empties waste baskets at his tasks
He has a dream of steak and beer in the evening.

Still men and women go about their work
Filling and emptying waste baskets. Then the rats?
Perhaps; I doubt it; rats do not value waste baskets
Unless they happen to possess, contain,
Apple peels, morsels of stale candy, crumbs of bread. (*M*, p. 324)

Something Slammed the Door To

It was the wind, nothing but the wind
That closed the door; return, breath, to the bosom.
Go to sleep again, simply, do not start,
Leave that to the red and eager heart—
Move on rhythmically, it was only the wind.

True, the hinge creaked, true, the door swung to,
True, the lock snapped, and then all was still.
But that was only the pressure of the wind,
The gentle wind that closed the door to the room
You came out of; it—was only the wind
You left behind you, that was only the wind—

Silence now, be silent, you have trudged
Many a mile to come to this, and drudged
Many an hour to gain this: be still now,
Breath and heart, oh, it was nothing, be still. . . . (*M*, p. 325)

These two sonnets fairly represent the consistent achievement of Moore. They are neither the best nor the worst, but average as observation and average as diction. Yet the one was most certainly put together, while the other one grew, in such a fusion of external with internal as Coleridge was talking about, in a creative imitation of nature rather than a mere copying of it.

I am aware that "The Contents of Wastebaskets" appeals to Henry W. Wells as one of "Moore's flirtations with surrealistic verse, where an ever-so-faint suspicion of symbolic meaning glimmers behind a foreground aggressively meaningless or nonsensical," in which Wells understands the contents of wastebaskets to symbolize "valuable truth looked upon by man's uncritical and unimaginative eye as unpromising refuse. . . . man's true history and inquiring mind (possibly even Moore's poetry) which is relegated to the scrap-heaps as unworthy of serious attention." *(Poet and Psychiatrist,* pp. 283-284). It is my belief that this interpretation reveals Wells' agility to extricate symbols more than it justifies Moore's poetic practice of "surrealistic verse." I have never been entirely sure what "surrealistic" means; if I do understand the term, however, I should have no objection to Wells applying it likewise to "Something Slammed The Door To," and if he did so, then I should repeat, here is an example of "surrealistic poetry" as opposed to "surrealistic verse."

I am sure that Moore was himself analytically aware of this hit or miss quality in his work, for he drew his own picture in the following sonnet:

Part Of Him Was Artist, Part Was Artisan

He saw a man die and made a vase of that,
He saw a child born and made another one;
Some of his vessels were made of clay glazed and baked,
Some of the rarer were carved out of elephant-bone;

He had a collection of them, all sizes and shapes,
Decorated all ways, never two the same—
Some had fabulous titles and many of them were
Totally nameless, completely without a name.

And sometimes he wove cloths instead of making pottery,
Sometimes he broidered and wove on a loom so large
It might have produced a sail for Cleopatra's barge
Or its produce might have been the prize at a lottery;

And sometimes, tired in the spring or in the fall,
He did absolutely nothing and never made anything at all. (*M*, p. 429)

The most interesting thing about this piece is what it does not include. The artist-artisan is represented as producing an immense variety of imitations of nature, but there is no indication that he is ever aware of anything but the superficial difference between "clay glazed and baked" and "elephant bone," the difference of "size and shape," of "titles" or "nameless," and of "cloths" as opposed to "pottery." He is aware of the fact that he is so carried away by his weaving that, to paraphrase Browning, his grasp exceeds his reach, so to speak. But he is nowhere presented as an artist aware of the difference between the creative imitation and the copy. He achieves both, if we may believe the poem's title, though in what relative proportions we do not learn.

Now, when I have said that Moore was analytically aware of this, I meant to imply that he was aware of it as an artistic problem, not wholly unrelated to himself as artist, and certainly applicable in some degree to every poet who ever wrote a line. It is characteristic of Moore, however, that he gives not only an oblique presentation of his problem in this sonnet, as well as in others, but frankly admits in his prefaces that his poems are "experimental" and "represent quick impressionistic efforts" *(Clinical Sonnets)* that they are *"Bastard Sonnets. . . .* born out of wedlock" *(Illegitimate Sonnets),* and are "a by-product of my daily activity" for which he "would prescribe a casual, conversational reading." *(From a Psychiatrist's Notebook).* In short, he vends his wares with a caveat emptor, so far as their being poetry goes. This we may approve as honest tradesmanship, but what shall we say when he implies that the essential poetry of the genuine poems is an "intrusion?"

Recurring to Coleridge's phrase about the conscious being "so impressed on the unconscious as to appear in it," note Moore on what apparently is, for him, the reverse of this process: "I find it difficult at times to separate realism from phantasy because symbols, despite my best intentions, often manage to get themselves into a poem. This intrusion of symbolism is especially noticeable in poems which, although stimulated by the external world of things seen and felt, seem to spring also from the inner world of feeling—sometimes from the subconscious." *(From a Psychiatrist's Notebook).* No, I do not discount Moore's humor at any time; perhaps he is being humorous here, but even so, with what? One must love one's bastard children no doubt, given the Olympian urge of Charles II to "scatter his maker's image through the land" physically, or Moore's titanic impulse to create bastard sonnets by the thousand. But when the perennial stud becomes the judge of his progeny and by implication does not recognize those faces which carry the true image of the-one-without-a-name, but dubs them "intrusions," we come face to face with the penalty of virility. It's a wise father that knows his own child, certainly, but any poet should know what a physician cannot avoid—the fact that there are children of light mingled among the criminals, idiots, and monsters who make up the "outer fringe" of society which at dead center is an undistinguished mass of commonplace but loveable citizens.

How flat is flat, poetically speaking? If the following sonnet, which incidentally, avoids the careless writing that Moore's admirers keep apologizing for, does not present an absolute absence of poetry, then I do not know what poetry is:

There is Money in Pornography

There is always money in pornography;
Even the small sums post card vendors get.

I have seen them in so many places:
Paris, London, Auckland, and Shanghai—

The tourist boat comes in, the tourists scatter,
Money in their pockets, and ideas
Of buying something in their sweet little minds

Something to take home, to show their friends;
They have saved for this, they expect to get
The most out of it; some are talking yet

About their ten days in Havana or Bermuda,
About the time he caught the barracuda;

They are natural prey for men who sell post cards
(Pornographic) to them by the yards. (*The Hill of Venus*, p. 70)

That pornography is a suitable subject for poetry I do not question. Nor do I have any doubts that the language of poetry is just what the subject demands to express its poetry, and need not, indeed should not, be the nearest approximation to "magic casements opening on the foam" that can be conjured up as window dressing. Simple words, bald words, crude words, trite words—any words will do, if the poet has a poem for which he properly needs them. Furthermore, I recognize the modern intellectual's fondness for flat statement as the proper and fashionable garb for "emotion," in contrast with the purple which "sentiment" so ignorantly wears. But I insist that line for line somewhere, in at least one line, or between the lines, or as an aura hovering, as not infrequently happens with a simple lyric, a poem about people who sell and who buy pornographic post-cards should be poetry, and for me there is not a hint or a vestige in "There is Money in Pornography."

Coming up the scale in the same book *(The Hill of Venus)*, we find what poetry amounts to at its crudest:

Galactic

They had one of these quiet relationships
In which neither one of them said very much
But all went smoothly, a well-oiled clutch
A well-greased axle, lots of motor fuel,
Nothing ever venomous or cruel
But much accomplished; it seemed effortless
A magical machine devoid of stress
A paragon of sheer productiveness
Amazingly converted at the start
From what had been a once-discarded part
But now a master turbine had become
Surpassing earth itself in spin and hum
Ordered somehow with the other stars
Secure beyond the pressure of their bars. *(Ibid.*, p. 29)

On a few pages, in a few lines, we find in this book that the poet in Moore can treat the theme of sex with genuine imagination. The best poetry in the book, unfortunately, seems to have "intruded" itself into reality in spite of Dr. Moore's best intentions, if we accept him at his word quoted above, but it has never quite assimilated the reality, nor been assimilated by it. Hence the anomaly of some excellent poetry in a poem which lacks composition. For example:

All telephone calls in this area cost ten cents
and you can get a lot of love for a dime

In the test tube of untried reality
The vermiform appendix of a blind date;

Such words refer to actuality,
Not abstraction, careless or sedate
Upon a dais, or a marble throne,
Seated, like a statue in the park

Where girls go out to use the telephone
Standing in a kiosk in the dark
That brings the hour, long awaited, for
The soldier or the sailor home from war;
Begun with coins, then the dial tone,
Soon an answer: "Yes, I am alone
The family is out; you may come over,"

The quick communication of the lover. (*Ibid.*, p. 9)

IV

I hope I have not pursued Coleridge's observation beyond the
point of no return, for I wanted it, not to illustrate that Moore is
not a poet, nor even that he is a bad poet, but rather that he is at
times a fine poet indeed. He is one of the few modern poets who
have written convincing poetry (to me at least) of love.

In writing love poetry, one lays himself open to more than
literary criticism; the ridicule that centers on self can never be
far removed from either the poet who writes of love, or the poet
who reads of love, because the lover's only self defense in love is
ridicule. The more sacred the rite and creed, and the greater the
immolation of martyrdom, the more ridiculous are the symbols
and the language to the eyes and ears of the skeptic self, yearn-
ing for martyrdom but unconvinced of its necessity.

Moore's love poetry displays this ambivalence constantly,
most fey when most serious, and most pious when most un-
believing. Of many illustrations of this I should like to cite
two—one in which the result is sustained poetry of a fine though
light quality, and the other in which the result is orthodox love-
piety of a rather low order, unsustained by poetic belief after the
fourth line.

Itinerary of Unwanted Song

With a burden of love now let my singing enter
Your door of bronze and plate glass, let it pass
The servants at the doorway of your house,
And pass your hall where visitors carouse,

And upon wings invisible let it rise
Up the grand staircase and beyond the eyes
Of butler and guests with drinking-glass fist-clenched,
And past their silly noses gossip-stenched,
Upstairs to your heart-room, to your boudoir
Where such song never has been sung before,

To find you absent, to find that you are not there
And nothing except the place where you comb your hair,
Except the empty dressing-mirror peering
At your empty cushioned dressing-chair! (*M*, p. 385)

Take This

I have no measure of my loving you,
But when you enter the room my speech is quickened
And when you leave a broad futility
Is draped upon the tables and the chairs.

With you to be near, to touch me, I am happy.
Absent—without you, a nameless void is made,
More real than the nescient oblivion
Where you are present, fatefully secure.

When you are gone the west is only the place
Where the sun goes down, the east is only
The region where it rises; but when you
Are here both are continually more and different.

Take and hold this dark heart, I beg you,
Always in your fast and certain fingers. (*M*, p. 395)

It is perhaps a great pity, but true, that frequently, Moore's best love poetry is such ironical, skeptical, but highly charged lines as "Old Lover's Claim" or "Will You Ever Pardon Me My Mistakes?" which record the disappointments and the failures of human love; the latter of these reads as follows:

> As far as I am concerned and you are concerned
> I am dead and my body has been burned
> And my ashes scattered out of an aeroplane
> Over the gardens by the ancient river
> As if they had been seeds of fruit or grain;
> And you are a sepulcher in a foreign land,
> Erected forgetfully by a foreign strand
> Though each of us is alive, and our hearts quiver
> If ever the other's name is heard or spoken,
> Because of promises we have made and broken,
> All for no reason, for no reason at all.
>
> How can I obtain, how can I ever obtain,
> Pardon? Not by prayer, I fear, for the stain
> Of my mistakes has fouled me like ox-gall. (*M*, p. 402)

This is Moore the poet at his colloquial, loosely rhythmic best. With the exception perhaps of "sepulchre" there is not a plush word in the whole, and the virtue of the sepulchre symbol is, like that of the seed ashes, too satisfying for one to quarrel with for the love of mere plainness. "Erected forgetfully" is a fair sample of what happens to Moore when "the conscious is so impressed on the unconscious as to appear in it"—a stroke of true genius. The only thing in the poem which seems to me to weaken it is the rime "foreign land" "foreign strand." In the sense of either there is logic, and "foreign strand" as antithesis of familiar "ancient river" is necessary perhaps, but both together seem justified only as a confession of poetic frailty.

This is about as close to perfection as Moore gets, except in such a poem as "Her Largesse." If any modern poet has plumbed deeper than this or found more satisfying language to record the experience, I do not know his work. I have not read a more profoundly conceived or a more perfectly imagined blend of imagery and passion. This is one of Moore's early *Fugitive* poems, for which I have searched his later work in vain to find an equal. Reprinted in several of his later volumes, it always stands up as one of the best in the book, as do in fact several others of his early *Fugitive* pieces.

Her Largesse

The kingliest parts of him belonged to her.

He'd given them to her once when she was ill,
Lamely, perhaps, and somewhat against his will.

But now she held them closely like a fur
Robe about her when the winds beat snow
Against her figure that had far to go
Over a road over a hill so steep
Those who reached its end could only sleep;

His long square forehead and his long-lidded eyes,
She held them tightly as a jockey holds
The reins wrapped over his knuckles in double folds
When the wind has beaten his cap down in his face
And this is perhaps the end of his last race
And to win it would be the key to paradise. (*The Noise That Time Makes*, p. 50)

About religion in its essence Moore has written some of the finest poems ever written by a skeptic, which means in my way of putting it, the best religious poetry, for the only conviction in words rings as an echo of doubt. What could be more ironical than that a gem of religious poetry such as this should have been written by one who cannot believe his own words? The wish is father to the thought even if not to the belief:

His Voice Is Like a Singing Tree

He spoke, and I climbed up into His voice like a tree
I could not fall out of, and there I slept.

Over my head the leaves, His sweet words, kept
Up a gentle murmur; at times they wept
Honey-like, and let fall great honeyed tears
To beat upon my drowsy-sweetened ears
That listened hungrily to the harmony
Of His sweet words, His tears and my poor fears.

Where should I have been? No other place,
Unless I were a mote to rest on His face!
Hidden in the foliage of His towering voice,
I could hear each cell that was part of me rejoice
With the greeting cry that angels are heard to use
When they leap to wipe Heaven's dust from His shoes. (*M*, p. 60)

As an act of pure imagination this is Moore at his best, but
among the numerous poems in which he traces his (and that of
most of us who would, if we could, believe) tragic (if it isn't I
don't know what is) lack of personal acquaintance with deity,
the following is an excellent example of what I have referred to,
perhaps too humorously, as his "incidentalism." It is also an example of Moore's best success with verse in which no symbols
"intrude" because they are the web of the poetic experience
itself.

And If I Would I Know Not Where To Hide Me

From my needs (of something to worship) that sit beside me
(When I travel alone—on railway trains)
And talk to those who populate inside me,
And all of us twiddle our thumbs and cudgel our brains
In brown studies as the world rolls by,
As the rails click and telephone poles flit by
And wires and fences rise and fall in the sky
And engines roar and rush incessantly—

And my needs of something to worship that run beside me
(When tired of sitting they run, and vice versa),
That treat me as a cashier or a bursar,
Saying: "Here is a penny!" or "Give us one
For God or the deity behind the sun!"
—Tragically and terribly they chide me. (*M*, p. 73)

V

Something should be said about the relationship of psychiatry and poetry in Moore's work. In fact, I wonder if psychiatry is not often responsible for what I suspect as charlatanry in his work, responsible, that is, because it has sophisticated the poet's necessary simple faith in the creative act itself. It is possible for a physician-psychiatrist to adopt in all sincerity the point-of-view of the relativist, skeptic, experimentalist, who proceeds empirically, but when the poet proceeds thus as a regular method, he constantly verges on the meretricious. Thus, the several hundred verses which obviously grow out of Moore's psychiatric practice are frequently marked by deep understanding of human nature, by sympathy, by humor, by common sense; many are memorable sketches drawn in language that is at the least acceptable and at the best practiced artisanry. I enjoyed reading them the first time, I have enjoyed reading them the second time, and I shall remember many of them for a long time. "She told me she had become a vaginal ear," "He said he was in a mood for angels but he never got to see them after all," "Locked in a prison with an invisible key," "He suffered from creative mentality," "He had something he wanted to give away," and others among the *Clinical Sonnets* are such good psychiatry that we may fail to appreciate their art, much as we purchase a ten-cents-store gadget for its usefulness and never note its design, frequently as superior in its way as anything accomplished by Praxiteles. And yet they are not poetry in the true sense that much, fortunately, of Moore's work is. The knowledge of a psychiatrist can produce, at its best perhaps, the following:

You Have Seen Them

Loiterers on the street, late, after midnight?,

Each is a story, a pathological novel,
An unwritten epic of frustration and despair,
Each has a tale to tell, invisible burdens
Weight down the shoulders of each one wandering there:

The prostitutes, pimps and perverts of post-midnight
In cities, the panderers and the panhandling ones
Frequenting the side streets off the main thoroughfares?

Each is a unit in a constellation,
Not a galaxy of brilliant successful stars
But a coal-pocket of dark sidereal junk
Material discarded from the universe,
The burnt-out residue of interstellar
Friction and collision and defeat. (*Clinical Sonnets,* p. 46)

But only the knowledge of the poet can produce this, which I
shall not predict to rest eventually among the immortal lines of
American, or world, poetry, but which I shall stake my whole
faith *is poetry:*

Lust and Silence

Lust grows out of silence, and in silence,
In the grave, lust dies and crumbles, falls
Into silence.
              Defeated triumphals,
Either part comes to silence when each one,
Started from a chair or bed by chance,
(This is silence) walks into a place
Where Time wears a mask and has no face
But hours, morning hours—evening hours
Different as different summer flowers.

Man or woman seated, standing, lying
Begets his lust—and lust will dart off crying
And run deep into silence, there to stop
Surveying valley depths and mountaintop.
Lust grows out of silence into silence. (*M,* p. 5)

To write thus is not learned, although it cannot be written
without learning. What one learns as a psychiatrist or as a poet
may be simply how to pretend to know and glibly to verbalize
with apparent conviction, as Moore has so well depicted in
"Pupil to Master":

Pupil to Master

I'm changed so you'd not recognize me now
(Randel said to Merlin), unless you happened to know
Me before I changed, as it happened that you did.
You remember how timid I was, and how I hid
When hags and hens or churls and carlines came
Asking you for advice, crying your name
Under your windows like prayers to the devil:
Well, they used to frighten me with their evil
Faces and eyes and tongues and eager fingers;
But now I look on them and my interest lingers.
I do not fear them since I've learned from you
How to counsel them as to what they should do,
To cool with my secret ice their hot desires,
Or how to warm them with my secret fires. (*M*, p. 139)

But one cannot learn from a teacher what the teacher does not
know so well as one knows himself, and this is what Moore discovers in "Lust and Silence," which no amount of psychiatry or
literary technique can account for. That he does not discover his
vein of poetry more often may, or may not, be entirely his fault.
I am inclined to believe that, considering the age in which he
lives, he has done better than his readers, and certainly better
than his non-readers, deserve. I, for one, am inclined to accept at
face value Moore's poetic confession that, in his own way:

No one has tried harder than I have tried
To catch the gleaming images that died:

Were they in the clouds, I caught them there,
And caught them in the flames two times as fair,
And in the earth in geologic straits,
And on the sea-waves where the seagull waits
For his reflection to return to him
That on bright days is bright and that is dim
On dim days on the water where he sleeps
Without a troubled conscience as he keeps
His head tucked in his wing and floats among

Seaweeds greener than the forest's song
At dawn, seaweed in winter that turns brown
And dies and to the ocean's floor sinks down. (*M*, p. 188)

One is especially inclined to accept such confession when it is preceded by another verse which invites the reader's critical scalpel both by what it says and the way it says:

If And When You Ever Buy My Poems

I will exchange the many that I dislike
For the few that you like; in other words,
You, for the few that you like, you will take
The many I dislike, then you will have both. . . .

It happened like this: my mind broke like a shard
And we piled the pieces up to make a path
From me to you, that you will grow to care
For the ones I did not care for when I put them there.

And, in time, I may even grow to love
The ones that you inscribed your name above;
And lastly, I become humility—
Which does not seem true, but my modesty
Is very present; what was and is yet to come
Is only a drop, a morsel, a scrap, a crumb, (*M*, p. 187)

For any student of the over 2,000 published sonnets of the estimated more than 60,000 filed away in Moore's papers in the Library of Congress, the poet's attitude toward his compulsive activity as a writer, and toward the creations which it has produced, is intriguing in its ambivalence. Although he tries to tell himself that it is just as natural and normal as a bowel movement and should be accomplished with no more aplomb and accepted without unnecessary fanfare, nevertheless, Moore both loves and hates the act of writing and the verses which it produces. This fact is borne out not merely by his prose comments on his works, but also by many of the poems which deal with his compulsion:

Sick of the noise made by my idle tongue,
My pen screech-scratching over an empty page,
I wish that I had never come of age,
If only in years, that I had never known
The trick that Cadmus learned when he scraped a stone
With another and sharper stone, that I had swung
Over the cliff of stillness with my body
That constantly issues noises vile and shoddy.

But nowhere I go does the evil dullness cease;
Into a forest or under a river's water
Still I keep company with Usna's youngest daughter
Who plagues my ears and will not leave me peace;
On through darkness, day and dusk and dawn
Still this wordage babbles on and on, (*M*, p. 300)

But on the other hand,

Do it, make it, be it—it will be named;
If there is shame in it you will be shamed. . .

But there it lies, at which the world will gape;
Or if it formless fall, there is content:
The tolerant way down which significance went;. . . (*M*, p. 120)

And undoubtedly, and humorously, the most horrible thought of
all, possible only in a bad dream, is that there must ultimately
come an end to such potency:

Plentiful? I?

I realized I was no more plentiful.
I was asleep in the port of coldest morning
When suddenly "How plentiful you are!"
Burst like the fragments of a shattered star.

It fell on my shoulders like the 4th of July,
Incandescent its sheen, iridescent I.
People complained: I wonder where we are?
This is unusual! So incorrigible!
These fragments of an energy that bursts
Ranging from the passable to worst.

But then I listened for the morning tones
Of bells, I heard some of the faintest ones

But ill they boded when there came a lull
That taught me I was no more plentiful! (*Clinical Sonnets*, p. 72)

After such knowledge, can one complain of the valley river, often muddy and full of debris, that it is not a clear stream welling thinly but consistently pure from the mountain side?

If Coleridge's opinion is valid that, "one character belongs to all true poets, that they write from a principle within, not originating in anything without," then most of Moore's variety, topicality, and apparent lack of commitment would seem to indicate that most of what he wrote merely accumulated. One can read all of Moore and never feel that one knows this poet as one knows Wordsworth, or T. S. Eliot (or Edgar Guest, for that matter), for Moore can get involved in almost any kind of game, showing his hand but one card at a time. He leaves his reader guessing what is yet left to play, and suspecting that there may be less (or more) in it than the poet is willing for us (or himself) to know at this stage of the game. Thus there are two (he has admitted to *Six*, as I am aware) sides to Moore the poet. One is completely outgiving and the other extremely inholding. He has stated the case himself:

I—Me—Je—Ego—Wo, Etc., Etc.
or
The Essential Autobiography of Myself

In one area I do not perform
Very well; I am below the norm.
It is in *the true giving of myself;*
Of course, I give a lot and try to give
Even more, but somehow I do not.
I am a cryptic volume on a shelf;
Few open me; few ever take me down
To read and fondle; I am isolate;
Self-containment is my tragic fate.

I did not ask or choose that it be so;
It was the only way that I could grow.

Small seed I was among those other seeds,
Planted in a garden among weeds.

But still I enjoy water and love the sun;
And, I know, I am not the only one
So molded that the fever of desire
In me is always channelled ever higher

Until it strikes the curtain of the sky;
Then, satisfied, I know that I shall die. (*A Doctor's Book of Hours*,
p. 157)

His "true giving of himself," where is it? Although in
retrospect I feel sure that some of Merrill Moore's sonnets will
be around a long time, if I were asked to select ten for posterity,
I should much prefer to select a hundred. That is an indication
both of my liking for them and of my feeling that I would be
much safer if I could choose a hundred, because there are few if
any perfect poems among them, and yet there are dozens which,
were they only perfect, or even more nearly perfect, would do
more for our day than Tennyson's perfect best (which was, after
all, in its day *perfect best*) ever did for his.

But considering all, it is as well
That art rejects, is rejected, and Time anoints. (*M*, p. 301)

I had chosen these two lines as epigraph to my article before
the writing of it began, in order to illustrate finally the incerti-
tude of Moore's poetic creed and belief, and to show how far his
scientific relativism and empiricism has detached him from
belief in his own truth. The fallacy that "Time anoints" is pure
myth of the rationalistic, skeptical, scientific variety so characteristic of our era. To set the record straight, it was not Time that
anointed Shakespeare and Wordsworth, but Ben Jonson and
Coleridge, and, in a smaller way, the host of believers in poetic
truth who have accepted with periodic modifications of dogma,
the original verdict of those high priests of literary art. Whether
William Carlos Williams, Louis Untermeyer, Dudley Fitts, or,
originally and most felicitously, John Crowe Ransom, should be
credited as being the most authoritative "anointer" of Moore, the
fact will remain.

THE POET AS COMPOSER—
LEE ANDERSON

I first became acquainted with Lee Anderson in 1953, when we negotiated an agreement for the benefit of the Library of Congress Archive of Recorded Poetry. At that time he was not only a poet whose work had received recognition among fellow poets, but an entrepreneur whose flourishing greeting-card business took him around the United States; and on these perigrinations he became a not-so-casual collector of tape recordings of poets reading their own works—that is, *when* his tape recorder could catch them. In addition to the Library of Congress, Harvard, and perhaps one or two other institutions, Lee Anderson was the principal pioneer in this work, and his splendid collection, now at Yale, remains one of the most important of its kind. This long labor of love has bearing on what follows, in that it was the practical outcome of Anderson's early conviction that poetry, in spite of Gutenberg, is still primarily an oral-aural art, and that a poet's rendition of his own poems should bring to the student of poetry an opportunity for enriched appreciation.

We had become friends and exchangers of family visits by the time he began work on his third long poem, *Nags Head.* As the weeks turned into months and the months into years (three plus), I was given opportunity to read and hear, part by part, a succession of working drafts, until I marveled at not merely the dedication and sweat of his labor but also the discretion with which he threw away fine phrases and whole lines in his quest for the poem he would at last send to the publisher. Sometimes I scarcely recognized the new version of a passage that a few months before had seemed somewhat more than adequately "finished." It was still thematically the same, but more carefully orchestrated in its overall effect.

Sometimes I felt his methods as composer were not above reproach for an occasional loss not offset by a gain. One such instance has remained so vivid that I requested the poet to resurrect the lost lines from his early draft to serve as an illustration in this context. The passage occurs early in Part I of *Nags Head*, following the lines which establish the poem's dominant metaphor,

> The trial and error chance
> Of death on a Nags Head dune—*

and splendidly set forth the ambiguity of life-force-death-wish in "other ways to wear the eye/the ear," as follows:

>   . . .when. . .as the hound willed the bird
> Within gun range from the underbrush
> The bird, between certain death on open field
> And the uncertain reach of sky
> Chose sky
> . . .when as the wings thrash
> Stayed your trigger hand, held
> Captive by the scorched wild
> Call as the cock names his fear
>   You wear his eye   his ear.

This passage as revised and published in *Nags Head* (1960) is indubitably improved upon, but with a great loss. Here it is:

>   . . .when. . .as the dog willed the bird
> Within gun range from the underbrush

* All quotations are by permission of the poet Lee Anderson.

> The bird   between certain death in stubble field
> And the uncertain reach of sky
> Chose sky
> . . .when as. . .the cock names his fear
> You wear his eye   his ear.

Anyone who has ever heard the pheasant cock's "scorched wild call" cannot but recognize the loss of the word "scorched" from the finished poem. One can applaud "dog" instead of "hound" (although Pennsylvanians hunt pheasants with beagles), and "stubble field" instead of "open field," and one can get along without "the wings thrash/stayed your trigger hand"; but "held/captive by the scorched wild/Call" is a loss hard to justify, "as the cock names his fear."

The time was 1955 and the place Anderson Farm, near Potosi, Pennsylvania, where the poet and his wife, Helen, had renovated (slightly) a typical frame farm house and endowed it with the principal appurtenances of a chateau—namely, a pond like that of Chaucer's Franklyn, with "many a breem and many a luce," and a wine cellar well-stocked with Anderson's own vintages, pressed each year by the master himself from sufficient tonnage of grapes red and white to keep his daily table in its Pennsylvania version of European style. Over a weekend we would fish, read and listen, wine and dine, in an extravagant simplicity devoted to pleasures personal and poetic, while I expanded my appreciation of the one quality of poetry to which I suspect most habitual readers today, even of poetry by preference, have never given more than a modicum of their attention.

Reading Lee Anderson for the first time was, and still is, like listening to fine music, without wholly understanding it, perhaps, or rather, without being aware that one understands what one enjoys, although one hears and detects something in the pattern of sounds that might have, really must have, meaning, if only one could find and seize the illusive thread and follow it out of the magic labyrinth one entered through the opening bars. This is a way of saying that his is one of the easiest modern poetries to read but perhaps one of the hardest to follow. It is also to say that there is frequently a pleasure in following se-

quential sounds and rhythms for their own sake, so strong that
it dispenses anodyne to sense, in spite of the contrapuntal
vividness of the images conveyed to the eye that would see what
it hears, but sometimes fails to, as sight and sound tend to fuse
into an experience that is wholly neither, as in the following
passage:

> grey is the dominant the dream tone
>   of the city of the artist
> the way these chords and phrases
>   of shade and light blend and repeat
>   soothes   and fires   like music
>   like music swelling   falling
>   the grey of a sailing barge and a gull's wing
>   of early pewter   and newly minted silver
>   the grey that sounds like a loon's call
>   the ring of thin glass
> and a smothered laugh in summer rain.

To recognize what the poet is doing (and how nicely!) is the
first duty of his reader, but after such recognition, what? One
must read on, of course, until the repeated phrases of "the
dream tone" wind down, after many sonorous intervening lines,

> in V-shaped diamond shafts of sun   aslant
> the bright dust-laden air above the street
>   the grey of wire-thin winter rain against
>   warm wool monotones of modest
>   in-between brownstone houses

and come to a pause with "a contralto laugh in summer rain."
   But what shall one think when the first passage, quoted from
Prevailing Winds as first published (by Conrad Aiken in *Twentieth Century American Poetry*, 1944), becomes finally, as it
appears in *Nags Head and Other Poems* (1960), abbreviated to

> Grey is the dominant   the dream tone
>   of the city of the artist
> The caprice of cloud and sun of   light and shade
>   Is newly minted silver   and the warm
> And Quaker monotone   of an Archaic Gothic cathedral.

And yet, the sequence still winds down to the "V-shaped diamond shafts of sun aslant" and ends in "a contralto laugh in summer rain." One may be tempted to think the composer did not know what he wanted to do the first time around (or the second or third), but was merely extemporizing variations on a theme, composed and recomposed, with the brain functioning more as a synthesizer than an organizer, and frequently, at the least, as a mere synthesizer of sounds and images which carry their own esthetic *raison d'être* up from levels below consciousness. The truth is, perhaps, that he did know as an artist knows, but had a hard time reaching his goal.

Well, isn't this essentially what most modern poets have done at their best, to a greater or lesser degree? Perhaps. But none quite so deliberately as Anderson, it seems to me, has set out to compose a music of words accompanied by images, rather than the other way around. And certainly none has in quite his manner let meaning tag along, as it can, like a little brother barely able to keep up with the older boys, or even falling so far behind that it catches up only later on. The experience of the poet as composer is, in Anderson, not essentially different from the experience in Eliot or Tolson, perhaps, or any true poet who uses words to some degree as a composer of music uses sounds; but in Anderson the experience is frequently most concentrated on sound as primary, image as secondary, and meaning as the illusive blend of both, reached perhaps, but not always grasped. And this is his truest poetry.

Thus Anderson's poetry is an extremely sophisticated creation, though from simple materials, for which a sophisticated audience is required. Not the sophisticated audience, however, that follows the theories and practice of a William Carlos Williams school, a Black Mountain school, an Eliot-Pound school, or any school of poetry. What Anderson needs is an audience that has learned to appreciate Whitman and Sandburg, as well as Pound and Eliot, and Aiken and sound-conscious novelists such as Henry James, and is willing to read by ear first and by eye second, or at least simultaneously. In any case, one doesn't dig line by line, or even sentence by sentence, as one may (but not necessarily) dig Eliot or Pound. Reading Anderson, one sails, so to speak, with the wind, along an ever varying shore.

Prevailing Winds is thus perhaps an ode or oratorio, in four sections, sonata form. Its theme is praise, praise of the esthetic principle (as opposed to the economic, ethical, or whatever), which the poet believes, or wants to believe, to be the principle of life. The four parts correspond to the "shape of a symphony," as the poet explained years later in "Notes Toward a Prosody for the Long Poem," published at the end of his *Nags Head* volume. They follow the seasons, and shift the scene from Manhattan to Gallatin, to Taghanic, and Stone Harbor, apparently in the fatal year of 1942, for the poem ends with the confrontation of war, on a note of affirmation, "life within life without end."

After more than a decade, his second long poem, *The Floating World*, appeared in *New World Writing VI* (1954). It was briefly introduced by a graceful note from Richard Eberhart, liberally utilizing Anderson's own explanations of what he was trying to do. Eberhart judged the accomplishment "one of the remarkable poems of recent years." He testified as a teacher of poetry: "It has so thoroughly captivated students of mine on both sides of the country that they wish to hear it over and over again."

The Floating World retained "within a square of four a structure of triads, roughly the shape of the symphony," as developed in *Prevailing Winds*, and further enriched the oral-aural effects of his earlier work. Into it, however, he introduced a dramatic quality and emphasis which marks this work as a sort of prolonged soliloquy, in which his non-tragic but equally self-conscious modern Hamlet, high up in a city office, alternately inside and poised on the window ledge, contemplates with oriental, philosophic suspension the pros and cons of life and death in a floating world. Life is sensuously and intellectually rich, but disappointment almost unbearable, as the man (the poet) considers the human predicament, the life force and the death wish between which a delicate "aesthetic equivalence" may counterbalance the impossibility of a "philosophical resolution of the dilemma," or so the poet hopes. Thus the esthetic theme of his earlier poem is dramatically elaborated, using three symbolic preoccupations, chosen by the poet for paper weights on his desk: figurines of Rhada, Buddha, and a race horse, Alvah R.

Out of the facts of life come poets' symbols thus—a fondness for the horse race, no less than Oriental religion!

The Floating World, like *Prevailing Winds*, is an autobiographical poem, a quest for, or better, a creation of, identity. Again the reader moves with the seasons from city to countryside, and back to the coast and the city. Out of this poetic quest, countered by a traveling man's business journeys and experiences, having arrived at a crisis in life, the protagonist richly meditates on the delicate balance by which he is able to live, and even compose this very poem, beginning:

> One step   no more   and by a step   no more
> To leap   to fall   and by that act to end an act.

And ending:

> Are you the beater or the beaten one?
>   You are the meteor hyphen between
> The sacred ritual of Rhada
> Sensuality and the Buddha passion
> Floodlighting the mind
> In a curious lifelong link
>   The rhythmic love dance gives
>   Our only answer to things as they are
>   Things which can never be
>   Resolved by reason
>   Simply.

> For this moment we know the laws
> Of our suspension.

In writing thus his own spiritual autobiography, however, the poet has remarkably projected the spiritual biography of modern American *Man*, among the ambiguities of his reality in a floating world. Yet it is not profundity that makes this poem remarkable, but its music, composed as the poet describes his practice, thus: "My own procedure is to 'score' four to eight lines at a time. I try to interrelate all the accented vowel and consonant sounds within a given group of lines, to tie in not an occasional pattern of internal assonance and consonance but every stressed syllable in nearly every foot so that each has an echo of one or more harmonic counterparts." What this practice produces in sound patterns on every page, with image patterns accompanying, and meaning threading its way toward something that falls into shape overall with the last words already quoted, may be illustrated by two contrasting passages from the poem's second section, "Deer Creek Valley." First a pastoral passage:

> Go   Love   where the orchards bloom
> In new green song and leaf
> Where apple petals are thumbnail small
> Are paper-thin and linen-soft
> The flourish of this blossom fleece
> —The dazzle of it seems unreal—
> Will leave you   Love   a little breathless.

Then, two pages later on, the somewhat archaic (for good reason in the context), aphoristic beauty of four lines "scored" no less musically in harsher tones:

> How strangely men their mindes chastise;
> They gain their wisdome country wise
> And then expend their lives in cities
> On city-spawned contrarities.

Poetry is what remains, of course, after the first, but even more after the twenty-first reading and listening; and it is by this test that one judges, not the poet's theory of poetry, or his technical excellence in performing that theory, but the overall memorable result. By "overall" I mean the entire poem. It is my belief that *The Floating World* is one of the few long poems in English written in the twentieth century which is memorable "overall."

A poet who confines his work almost completely to long poems cannot easily be represented in anthologies; and for this reason Anderson remains, and perhaps may continue to remain, practically unknown to the vast majority of poetry readers, who come to modern poetry either as students or casual paperback browsers, through the perennial "new" editions of the essentially unchanging collections. Yet it may be hoped that some editor one day will wake up to the fact that four or five of the finest short poems published by an American poet since World War II are also his. Of all World War II poems, I think Anderson's "D. Jones' Locker" is likely to remain, along with Karl Shapiro's "Elegy for a Dead Soldier," the most memorable, a truly noble poem. "Ski Tow" is superb musical and metaphorical composition. "The Room of the Four Treasures" and "Ice Boat and Flight" achieve as personal lyrics the very essence of all that is genuinely poetic in a "confessional" poem, which is alleged to be the genre most typical of this age. It may be hoped that an anthologist will someday discover them.

Nags Head (1960) again employed architectonics of the symphony for poetic organization, but this time, I believe, with a less insistent musicality in its progressing patterns. A stream of consciousness progression in the poem largely takes over. It is a layered stream, even as the poet's personal existence is layered in currents moving now at top, now lower, and sometimes very close to the river bed, with eddies and cross currents at every point in time-space. Imagination is constantly at work, sometimes at the surface, sometimes lower down, as the poet takes from his reading and philosophical speculation some of the images, metaphors, and symbols of the poem's progression. Personal existence is also constantly at work, but rising to the surface or diving, as the poet takes other imagery as metaphor and symbol from his daily "reality," chiefly from home and love life. The deepest current is usually the subconscious mythical, which never wholly surfaces, but sometimes comes very close as it obeys the law of esthetic gravity, as it were, and moves toward the inevitable revelation.

This poem is, like its predecessors, broadly, if symbolically, autobiographical, allusive and abrupt in its transitions, within the mind's eye shifting from the purely imagined to the actually (sensually) experienced (which is *not* to say "unimagined" of course), as the poet makes with words the synthesis that becomes a poem of his will to live, symbolized overall in the metaphor of man's will to fly. The first "movement" begins with the protagonist as sole passenger in a plane, grounded in "The Painted Desert" (as the first movement is titled) by the pilot in a last act before death. The passenger is thus confronted with the alternatives of death, or of "willing" himself to fly, wholly untaught except by example of the Wright brothers who first successfully by act of imagination, willed to fly at Nags Head. Willed flight becomes the unifying, heroic metaphor of the poem, as the protagonist lifts off the desert floor and flies to his green coming down on the "Susquehanna," (as the last movement is titled). The intervening parts, or movements, are "New Year's Eve" and "Potosi." "New Year's Eve" is a love poem, as boy meets girl at the Time's Square New Year's Eve ritual. "Potosi" is a lyric "Minuet-Trio-Minuet" movement, vividly scored to the erotic ambiguities of the life-force-death-wish battle of sex. This is certainly the most sombre of all the love sequences in the several poems, and as such lends conviction to the green-water symbolism of the protagonist's coming from the desert place of death back to life, in the concluding section "Susquehanna."

Bearstone, the fourth, and as yet unpublished, of Anderson's long poems, brings the poet's quest to a kind of resolution, if not conclusion. "The Silver Mine," first part in Anderson's customary four part structure, opens with the protagonist trapped in an abandoned mine, from which there is no escape save by a helping hand. This symbolic beginning, as in the earlier poems, is at once autobiographical and perhaps sociological, myth both of individual man and of mankind. The poet has described it in a letter thus: "The most enduring matrix of literary form is the paradigm of tomb resurrection, of lone man in the desert and his return to the garden, to woman as water as dream, to release from the cave into the flowering of the natural world." But with the theme of racial conflict adding still another current to the complex flow of man's fate, this final work in the tetralogy, one discovers, has moved from the private, lyric emphasis of *Prevailing Winds*, through the dramatic of *The Floating World*, and the heroic of *Nags Head*, to what seems an approximation of the epic mode, or at least a modern attempt at it.

As Anderson's comment has it, *Bearstone*

is a variation on 'the epic journey'. . . . *Bearstone* is not a play, it is not narrative, it is a conjugation of lyric and 'theatre' elements, of interior dialogue, voices off stage and on, of 'stills' where the only motion is the mind's and of incidents presenting confrontations in ultimate and radical conflicts: an insoluble conflict of will between races, one race holding another captive unwilling to grant either autonomy or the complete fraternity of a free society. . . . And though it is satisfying to affirm the will to live, to give an 'everlasting yea' to life even in a crippled plane *(Nags Head)*, the role to be assumed is that of the man who survives the prison of the silver mine *(Bearstone)* only by the hand of another. In the last section of the tetralogy, 'The River Steamer Pocahontas,' the task for the protagonist is to reconcile the conflict of men, the hostility and struggle for supremacy between races...."
(Letter to the writer)

And, as in the earlier poems, the protagonist is at once the poet and mankind.

At this writing, *Bearstone* is still undergoing the poet's painstaking revision and recomposition—perhaps the most difficult and potentially the most exalted of all his work to date. I have read and reread it with great pleasure. Whether it will equal or, for me, excel the success of repeated readings of the earlier poems in the tetralogy remains to be seen. I am not yet convinced by its final part. In any event, the composer's skill is as evident as of old. The lines are music to the inner ear, and the imagery memorable, even when the "message" knells a sad truth that denies, in effect, the whole esthetic upon which Anderson has seemed to stake his poetic claim:

> The horn and siren   are
> The only dial tones the city-deaf can hear:
>> Three dozen adults   death voyeurs
>> Peep down at rasp and thrust of knife
>> In hour-long rape of steel in flesh.
> Who answers the woman's screams?
>> None   not one.

This is not merely a modern ethical problem to ponder; it is an esthetic problem as well. For who listens anymore, really? And who can see and know what he sees unless he also hears? In the realm of poetry, even the best of our poet-critics seem largely tone deaf, because their education has been chiefly by sight. This is true even of those who sometimes confess their weakness as readers, unintentionally as did Randall Jarrell in his admission concerning Sandburg, "It is marvelous to hear him say *The People, Yes*, but it is not marvelous to read it as a poem." This may or may not be laid at the door of John Ransom's Nashville born "new criticism," but it is a sad fact that our best critics of that school have not been noted for their educated ears, even when, with Jarrell, they can recognize the quality of free verse when it is performed by a master of the oral-aural art.

Thus, not all the painstaking talent Anderson lavished on *Prevailing Winds* and *The Floating World* could commend them to, or defend them against, the casual violence of critic James Dickey's ridicule—an ex-night-fighter pilot's unspent fury after more than a hundred missions guarding bombers unloading bombs on Orientals more than a decade before. Opined Dickey, "Originality makes a truly monumental absence over these poems, and most darkly upon the elaborate paste-up 'masterpiece' 'The Floating World.' This last is surely one of the most cold-bloodedly over-serious concoctions ever released to public scrutiny. . .the absolute and unchallengeable *reductio ad absurdum* of cultural-revery poems. . . ." ("From Babel to Byzantium," *The Sewanee Review*, Vol. LXV, No. 3, Summer 1957, p. 525). One suspects an element of fear in such critical overkill, fear not only of "cultural-revery" but also of the philosophic artistry which perceives "The act of love as ritual," no less than as junk-yard fucking, but above all the fear of music that cannot be understood by an ear attuned to hillbilly.

I think the scientific evidence is overwhelming that modern man is losing ground aurally, if not morally, and who can be surprised, with the air as well as the land swarming with deafening noise? No wonder the music of this generation (*Hair, et al.*) is several decibels louder than the sirens on the street; perhaps the young can't hear any other kind. Neither Archibald MacLeish nor Mark Van Doren could be more than half heard, even with heavy amplification, in their tributes to Sandburg at the Lincoln

Memorial on September 17, 1967, while the jets from National Airport screamed overhead. And I can testify that during the eighteen years I have been arranging poetry readings in the Coolidge Auditorium of the Library of Congress, despite almost yearly improvements in our audio amplification equipment, the audience progressively maintains that the poets cannot be heard in our small auditorium. It would seem that we may be rapidly reaching the day when whatever flashes on anyone's inward eye that mirrors the Wordsworthian "bliss of solitude," will be as merely visual as it has always been for those born deaf. Preferably, perhaps, only the violently visual, at that—minus the screams! While these developments may be inevitable, they only serve to reinforce a disability that educators have remarked for more than one generation: namely, that the span of listening attention is usually far less, even for the bright child, than the span of reading attention. It was truth, even if only part truth, that Robert Frost saturninely muttered to me before going on stage before an SRO audience: "Most of them don't come to hear me; they want to say they *saw* me."

What, then, shall I say about Anderson's remarkable essay, "How Not to Read Poems—A Dissenting View" (*Art and the Craftsman*, Harned and Goodwin, eds., New Haven and Carbondale, 1961)? I can only agree with him that 1) "The significant problem is how to find an adequate audience for poets." 2) "It is wrong to *see* a poem before you hear it." 3) "It is the sensuous pressure of syllables in ordered progression that gives us pleasure." 4) "Listening to poetry is the first rule of the game. . . . There is no substitute for hearing a poem if you are going to poetry for enjoyment rather than intellectual exercise. Anything less than verbal communication is a violation of the nature of the medium. . . . It is somewhat like looking at a pretty girl's hand instead of holding it. . . . The answer is long playing records, reading aloud in the living room, reading in dormitories and in small groups. In the last resort one can read aloud to oneself." Hence, one cannot be surprised that Anderson's recording of *Nags Head* (Yale Series of Recorded Poets, 1960) exemplifies splendidly all that he has said on this subject.

But alas, who will hear the poet? The popular "poetry" of the

Beatles and their ilk demonstrates that, for the young, words with music today are only primitive grunts or wails to be repeated on almost every beat, dozens of times, as mere accompaniment for the strident music, carrying only the most elementary, infantile messages of emotion. On the other hand, the splendidly sophisticated "concrete" poetry of the cement school appears to be sculptured for the deaf by the deaf. And the school of "breath" poetry, taking to heart Hamlet on the ease of playing the recorder, "give it breath with your mouth, and it will discourse most eloquent music," frequently sounds to me very much more like over-aged panting than like poetry, though it looks on the page much like the scissored prose that still another school maintains is the *poesie nouvelle.*

Nevertheless, "he that hath ears" may find Anderson's poems among the truly memorable compositions of this era. But what is memorable to any of us? One supposes that nearly any poet would agree with Robert Frost's remark that he hoped to have made at least a few lines that men would not be able to forget. But what is likely not to be forgotten? What one should remember? What one wants to remember? Tries to remember? Or what one simply can't help remembering, for whatever reason, itself lost to memory—as for me, the "scorched wild call" of the pheasant remains, though lost to the poem, after more than a decade? Any poet sophisticated about his own memory, his own reading, his own writing, who has made a single phrase *con amore,* knows in his heart that this so carefully cultivated blossom will perhaps fare no better in the long run of man's rank green or sparse desert memory, than some wild oat that fell in a for-the-moment less crowded, or simply more fertile, ground. Will anyone remember anything of Frost, or of Shakespeare for that matter, if one listens only to the likes of McKuen's *Stanyan Street,* even at its best—"The freckled morning/moving into day now"—or on a somewhat different plane, O'Hara's "While she whispered a song along the keyboard/to Mal Weldron and everyone and I stopped breathing"? The answer, I think, is obvious. But suppose one listens to these, plus, perhaps, Roethke's "What's madness but nobility of soul/At odds with circumstance?" And then suppose one projects oneself in imagination into the next generation, or century, and finds, by chance, all three anew? Then what's likely to be memorable?

In poetry it is not the experience, real or imagined, however vivid and/or excruciating. It is only the words that a poet found, which say at least as much, and quite possibly more, to the reader then. And if it be said that such brief quotations as those I have just used never represent the poem or the poet at his memorable best, then I say with confidence that the same quality of memorableness (or lack of it) will convince any reader equipped for memory, if he reads in entirety all three of the poems from which I have just chosen these lines.

Now, I should be less than frank if I left the impression that McKuen's "Day Song/Night Song" or O'Hara's "The Day Lady Died" were not memorable enough at least to cause me to go back and look them up for a second reading, for the purpose of illustrating my point in this essay. In the first case, when I looked over *Stanyan Street* originally, and asked myself if there was a line of real poetry in it, there was only one line, and that's possibly why I remembered it at all. On the other hand, I doubt that I would ever have sought even this second reading for either of these "poems," except that I wanted them for illustration. With the line and a half from Roethke, however, I did not have to go back to the book. I remembered it after several years, and, of course, more than one reading. There are many lines in Anderson's poems which, like the one from Roethke, I cannot easily forget, such as the closing lines of "Ski Tow":

> Aimless he seems flying through fir
> Goggles   mittens   skipole   and skull
>   Challenging the forest to throw
>   Hemlock in the path of his skill
>
>   Skillfully with aplomb of swallow
> Threading evergreen needle and cone
> From summit of run to meadow willow
> He is your shadow   and mine   and vain.

But, as I have said earlier, it is my belief that Anderson has written some of the very few long poems in our day which are memorable "overall." His word music is certainly a quality

which enforces this belief, but there is something more. St. John
Perse has said that the "realm which poetry explores is that of
the soul and the mystery in which human beings are enveloped."
Anderson's exploration and his findings, indeed not unlike
Perse's own, are what make his poems memorable overall for
whoever has ears to hear and eyes to see. At least that is my
judgment after many readings of the earlier poems and several
readings of the manuscript of *Bearstone,* as well as two listen-
ings to Anderson's tape recordings of this final poem in the
tetralogy. Each time he comes through better than ever. There
are not too many poems of today, long or short, of which I can
say that repeated readings give, each time, more and more.

A LETTER TO ALI BABA

The invulnerable smile of the abstract
Is spread across the past,
A cobweb's pattern of acquiescence
Covering the Holes of Calcuttas;
Experience is a door in the ages
Formidable and delicately balanced,
As Ali, the ace Individual,
At the wall of the answers mutters.

"Ali Baba and the Forty Thieves"—Oscar Williams*

I

Mr. Ali Baba
000 Madison Avenue
New York, N. Y.

Dear Ali Baba:—Do you remember the little Jew, almost a dwarf but more of a gnome, who grew up some fifty years ago, on occasion scared nearly to death, in your East Side slums? I mean the one who wrote such flamboyant poems (one about you), and who became the truest bard of your megalopolis. How

---

* All quotations are from *Selected Poems*, Scribner's, 1947.

he sang, of his terror and alienation, and of the peculiar beauty he found in your denatured landscape!

He was a complete pretender, Ali, but the theatricality of his honest pretense was the only means by which he could defy hypocrisy in the world he (and you?) loved and hated, mid-twentieth century. Like you, he was a New Yorker for real. Remember, Ali, you were to him "the ace Individual"! What was he to you? I am going to try to guess your answer.

Being born a Jew in Russia, from the earliest childhood he recalled indistinguishable nightmares of real and imagined persecutions, the goyim scarcely less terrible than a tyrranous father, who slaved to transport wife and children to America but exacted in return their complete submission. Unlike the pants-presser father, his permissive mother had enjoyed "advantages," a cultured, literary upbringing. From her he drew his belief in ideal beauty and his passion for poetry. This passion was nourished by a succession of female teachers, whose pet he regularly became with the ease that belongs to the imaginatively gifted Josephs of all races. As a physical specimen he would remain somewhat funny by male standards, but he seems never to have lacked for female devotion, seemingly out of proportion to any other merit than the degree with which he returned it, on occasion, "by fiat of adoration."

In consultation with one of his adoring females, a younger sister, he decided while still in his teens to abandon his family name. The poems which he so regularly placed in the mail so certainly came back, in spite of their obvious (to him) genius, that there could be only one possible explanation—the flagrantly Jewish name of their author! Characteristically perhaps, he chose the name of a current matinee idol who was then playing in a movie serial entitled "The Goddess." When an often-rejected poem was accepted on its first trip out over the magic adopted name, there was born a poet's identity, Oscar Williams.

Under this literary alias, he so completely abandoned his past that only on his deathbed, nearly half a century later, would he reveal to close friends how, in his own words, he had lived "a complete phoney," but with little or no regret. One of his most incredulous friends, himself of Russian Jewish heritage, could only express amazement that not once in a dozen years had Oscar admitted by the flicker of an eye to acquaintance with Yiddish, Hebrew, or Jewish customs, which might have betrayed him as an erstwhile insider now outside by choice. Some may have suspected, but few, if any, penetrated that alias without Oscar's acquiescence.

There were possibly some among the considerable number of literati assembled for his Episcopalian funeral service who would have agreed with Oscar's own verdict of "phoney," particularly if they had known the facts, however different their literary reasons might have been. But few among them would have questioned his devotion to poetry, which he was accustomed to insist on, as the primal and primary art. Even those with whom he quarreled and spoke of spitefully, as they sometimes were wont to speak of him—*enemies* is hardly the word for such literary opponents—had to admit the countless proofs of his dedication, if not of his talent. He not only encouraged innumerable would-be poets, many of whom achieved some recognition, he also did all he could to get them paid well for their work. He was a salesman for poetry, whether his own or that of another whose talent he espoused, soft sell or hard sell, every day of the week, every week of the year.

It was not infrequently alleged that he pushed his own poetry to an obnoxious degree. Ali, who has known a poet who did not push his own poetry, on occasion, by whatever means, and to an obnoxious degree? If Oscar was never less than completely obvious in his salesmanship, it may be said that he was perhaps the only completely honest person in this respect who ever attended a literary cocktail party. Who can forget the little peddler with his shopping bag full of paperbacks? Ali, the publishers of his millions of poetry anthologies should erect a monument, in simple gratitude, to the poetry salesman without peer!

But he was first a poet, as he conceived himself, and Ali, I think you should do something about this, for he wrote primarily *about* you, and *to* you, even when you wouldn't read his poems.

II

As you may have guessed, Ali, the biographical sketches of Oscar Williams appearing in such reference works as *Twentieth Century Authors*, as well as in various reviews, are a mixture of fact and fiction, to which Oscar seems deliberately to have contributed quantities of both, for his obvious reasons. His identity as a poet was "all that mattered"; he disavowed any other identity; he willed to exist only as he conceived himself. If this was charlatanry, then make the most of it, so long as it was in the great cause of poetry, the only thing that was really real. The biographer who eventually must fill in the factual gaps and reduce the fictions will surely have his work cut out for him. In brief, however, I will tell you what I've learned, Ali, since Oscar's death.

Oscar Kaplan was born in the Ukraine, at Staraya Sinyava, in December 1900, or possibly 1899. As indicated by the 1910 U. S. census, his father and mother may not have been entirely sure which year, since his was the only age not listed among those of the other six members of the family. The Kaplan family migrated to New York in 1908, and Oscar, the eldest of the children, went promptly to school. When he was 17, following his mother's death, he was taken out of high school and put to work "trimming coats." Very shortly he left home to live by himself, holding various odd jobs, until his identity as the poet "Oscar Williams" became established by the publication of some early poems. Whereupon he is reported to have quit working, and to have been supported by the younger of his two younger sisters, who earned her living as a typist. In 1921 his first book of poems, *The Golden Darkness,* was published by Yale University Press, inaugurating The Yale Series of Younger Poets. When he was twenty-two he met Gene Derwood, a young woman from Peoria, Illinois. They were married some time later, and both worked for a time in a sporting goods firm by the name of Davega's, where he eventually came to be in charge of advertising. This employment lasted until 1930.

During this period he completely abandoned poetry, but gained considerable affluence. He seldom referred to these, or to the next half dozen, years, preferring to emphasize the later period (1937 ff.) of his "unsuccessful starvation" as a poet. This was the time from which all, or nearly all, of his acquaintanceships in the literary world were dated, and during which he began writing poetry again. Perhaps all that is poetically essential to know about those earlier years is what he wrote in his "Purely Personal Poem," or as he later title it, "Autobiographical Note." It begins "When I crawled out of the padded pit of the commonplace. . . ."

Publication in 1940 of *The Man Coming Toward You*, with W. H. Auden's sponsorship, brought mixed praise from the likes of Alfred Kreymbourg and Stephen Spender, but sharp derogation from nearly everybody else who reviewed it. Neither *what* the poems said nor *how* they said it suited the reviewers' taste. What they disliked most was just what Oscar tried to do, to portray the civilization he knew in an idiom poetically distilled from the advertising hoopla that predominantly characterized it. What they missed, or misconceived, was the validity of his vision of megalopolitan man in the years that led up to World War II, and those who, like Louise Bogan, did not misconceive it, "still did not like it."

With the publication in 1945 of Oscar's next book of poems, *That's All That Matters*, Conrad Aiken almost alone among reviewers found generous amounts of praise to bestow. But publication the following year of *A Little Treasury of Modern Poetry* brought general praise for Oscar's skill as an anthologist and established his position as a literary power to be reckoned with—a status from which his creativity never recovered, as he became, once again, a relatively affluent advertising man, albeit this time in a better cause.

What had happened between the imitative and derivative poetry of *The Golden Darkness* of 1921 and the strident, garish, and theatrically original poems of *The Man Coming Toward You* was now undone. His *Selected Poems* appeared in 1947, to which little of significance was thereafter added, although praise from reviewers now became a thing somewhat more accustomed, to what extent a derivative of his power as anthologist one can only guess.

III

The quality of his poetry perhaps derives to a limited extent from Harte Crane, whose work he admired, but more from Dylan Thomas, whom he adored, adopted, and felt somewhat possessive about (as did others!). His favorite means of communication was a postcard photo of Dylan and himself, bearing a hurried scrawl on the verso. But from both Crane and Thomas, he merely took off on his own pyrotechnic trajectory, at times scarcely under control.

His poetry is always a poetry of contrivance and artifice. There is nothing "natural" about what he says or how he says it. Even the banality is a contrived Manhattanese, effectively adapted to his theme and purpose. His imagery tends to theatricality and carries the "punch" of advertising copy, distilled, however, to poetic proof from the sour mash of the thing itself. But above all, it sings, with syncopations and cacophonies appropriate to its theme, and remains memorable after twenty or more years. How much of the poetry written in the thirties and forties does?

His is a world of the living, breathing macabre, where "Man in his fatal hunger knows no death/So deep as the abyss within his hand. . ." where "the padded pit of the commonplace" is "thick with adults like. . . the man with the diseased hands hidden in gloves/Who wrote advertising to while away the split-second decade. . ." and where "The world's philosophies clack, like loose shutters. . . "— "Inside the structure with the cellar/Windows at which horizons drink like deer. . ." It is a terrible world, but beautiful with artifice and contrivance, its reality being its makeup, incredible ingenuity of the human mind, Manhattan, leviathan of makebelief!

Poe's dream world of croaking ravens, dark tarns, haunted palaces, lady corpses suspended between life and death, and countless images of infantile impotence in settings of the many-colored valleys of hysteria, gives way in the Williams nightmare of reality to "the breath of the everyday. . ./Churning up a cloud of coffins above the advancing pistons," where among "the angel-eyed neons and the asphalt asphodels," "a bird in the girders laughing immensely. . . checks in its orchestrations on the time clock," where "The sackcloth of martyrdom shines like a coat of mail/And there are guns up the sleeve that sleep on the breast," and "The lady with the glass torso/And the wooden face of nowhere/Is waiting for you. . . ."

There are several poems in which the quality of wide-awake, realistic nightmare reaches or surpasses, for a modern equivalent, Poe's nineteenth century rococo gothic at its best, and I think they may tell us something of the Williams psyche, just as Poe's tales and poems tell of his. For purposes of critical appreciation, however, the first thing one must do is recognize the poems for what they are. A number of Williams' critics have fallen into the same error that tripped James Russell Lowell's judgment of Poe in the *Fable for Critics*, into assuming that the "two-fifths sheer fudge" was not poetry because it did not make the kind of sense that poetry (Lowell's kind) should make.

Two of Williams' best poems are of this type—nightmares of his waking world transposed into poetic dream imagery—"The Leg on the Subway" and "The Horse of Accident." In both, the dominant anxiety is of senseless movement through space, "cornered in a moment out of time" on a subway train or a city bus, trapped and helpless, at least momentarily, in the bowels of machine monsters of a modern mythology, which have replaced the fabled Chimeras and Gorgons of old. The secondary anxiety is of a beastly non-human, non-self, the "other," seductively feminine in "The Leg on the Subway" and repulsively masculine in "The Horse of Accident." In either case, the dream image of terror is the near presence of an encroaching other that threatens self, with lust or fear. The humor which saves both poems from the infantile bathos that sometimes defeated Poe's horrors even at their best, is sufficient in "The Horse of Accident" to bring a quick, rational denouement: "It was not Centaur, Houyhnhmm nor progeny of both,/But the clear sheer head of the damned long ago/ Rearing as through a manhole the fury of its sloth." But this denouement scarcely diminishes the terror at the encroachment of one's modern fellowman.

In "The Leg on the Subway," a master's touch enabled Williams effectively to surmount the architecture of his contrivance and produce a denouement worthy of the climax. When "the long tongue of the earth's speed" suspends its licking of the pink leg to slip "hurriedly out through a window," the poet remains in his trance to "perceive" what he has "seen."

> I perceived through the hole left by the nail of the
> > star in my mind
> How civilization was as dark as a wood and dimensional
> > with things
> And how birds dipped in chromium sang in the crevices
> > of our deeds.

These lines will as surely survive as anything any American poet ever wrote, in my opinion, a perfect metaphor of the metropolitan human condition at mid-twentieth century. And if the poem to which they provide conclusion is not a masterpiece, then nothing written by an American poet in the last half century is likely to prove to be.

Anyone who ever talked or argued with Oscar Williams about religion could not escape the fact that his conversion to Christianity was sincere, if not devout. He was, of course, incapable of devotion, except to poetry. It was this sincerity that led him to hope that his religious poems might carry more weight than they do, or perhaps could. The mystery of the Christ may be in no wise enhanced by the pious and mournful numbers of T. S. Eliot, but neither is the mystery either beautified, deepened, or elucidated by a modern Byzantine surrealism such as the Williams vision of "The Last Supper." Perhaps the reason may lie in the reader rather than in the poet, because as phrased in an earlier poem "Ours is a last supper, without disciples." But I think not. What attracts the modern poet, and therefore the modern reader, if he is attracted at all, is the beauty of the Christ story, not its truth. So Williams is perhaps at his best in this, when his religious vein runs closest to his imagination's heart, as in "By Fiat of Adoration," when God "comes over into being. . ."

The modern religious poet's problem, ensconced in the past, Williams best put in his poem "On Meeting a Stranger in a Bookshop," as the two who have become, temporarily, "angels," say goodby "to the problem there in its track," and "The books tumble on our heads and we are buried." But even in their relative failure to stand up as twentieth century religious poetry, Williams' religious poems seem to me to serve this era far better than the maunderings of beat gurus or the pseudo-Hopkinsian plaints and pieties of "mod" Catholics, in that their idiom is still poetry even when it carries today no more religious conviction than does "In Memoriam."

What I have called the "denatured" urban existence provides Williams some of his most memorable and horrible, and occasionally horribly funny, images: the boys in "Picture Postcard of a Zoo" watch "next to the cage in which the Yak will die. . . the Zebra's yardlong idling. . ."; the shopper in winter looks at a frozen ox tail in the butcher's shop and thinks of "the cow's tail, how all summer long/It beat the shape of harps into the air"; the children in "Audience," ". . .with their townclock masks/ Laugh an adult laugh or cough a grown up cough." Truly, the poet wonders: "This undoubtedly is life, and there isn't a soul that wants it that way." But it is capable of becoming poetry, and he proves it.

Perhaps of several poems treating the theme of this denatured urban existence, the best, or certainly one of the best, is "The Praying Mantis Visits a Penthouse." In the poet's habitat, the pathetic insect's natural disguise, "its length of straw," escalates into an image of terror, and the poet seizes a stick to stop "This Martian raid distilled to a straw with legs." Although the Mantis prays "to the stick twice armed with Man," prayer is of no avail. The stick descends, and the Mantis spreads "The many colored pennants of its blood/And hugs my weapon. . ."

As the poet knocks the stick against the railing's ledge, dislodging the insect "into the gulf," he searches his mind "for possible wounds" and feels "The victim's body heavy on the victor's heart."

And what about man in this denatured existence? The title poem of Williams' 1940 volume begins "The man coming toward you is falling forward on all fronts." The paradox of civilization is set forth in the rest of the poem as bitterly as any poet has ever phrased it, to conclude, nevertheless, that "The man coming toward you is marching forward on all fronts." But Williams is not at his best as a sociological, and certainly not as a philosophical, poet. He is best when he conjures for our time, perhaps for all time, images that haunt the mind. "But nobody spoke, though all the faces were talking silently,/As the train zoomed, a zipper closing up swiftly the seam of time."

IV

After Oscar Williams' death in 1964, Ali, there was no memorial gathering of any clan of poets to sing his praise at Yale, where his first volume was published. He had no clan or clique. It is true that his friend George Barker wrote a somewhat senti-mental elegy, published in *Poetry*, and God knows *owed* him one. But there has been no volume of tributes. The establish-ment of poets generally affected to look down on him, and with-out the establishment where is one to be critically acclaimed?

Randall Jarrell, whose more recent death provided the proper occasion for just such an establishmentarian memorial service, and for essays galore (now collected in a fine volume), perhaps indicated best just why this was. In remarking on one of the many Williams anthologies, from which he as well as a number of the other establishmentarians had been omitted, Jarrell observed that Thomas Hardy's poems occupied about the same number of pages as the anthologist had allotted to his own poems. Jarrell's acid comment was to the effect that an anthol-ogist must think quite a lot of his own poems to give them equal space with Thomas Hardy!

And Williams did think very well of his own poems, and if he had given them any less space than he gave Thomas Hardy's, he would have been, in his own egotistical view, a dishonest anthol-ogist. He may have been, probably was, frequently a mistaken anthologist, but he was not a dishonest one.

On looking back now, Ali, at that anthology, and at those of Hardy's poems included, in comparison with those Oscar allotted to himself, one wonders. Maybe, who knows?

In any event, Oscar is your true Manhattan poet, Ali, singing of cyclopean artifice, in the babel of contrivance, which he knew so intimately and terribly. He loved "Mrs. Nobody going nowhere for a token" and feared "the bestial scorched neck" of his "fellow passenger from senseless space." He wanted so much to cry out "I belong to you, amongst you, I am one of the human race," but he wondered "why is it so hard?" And he knew there was for him only one "Knuckle knock on finality, sing, bird, sing."

Finally, Ali, I should not have to tell you how much he admired *Ali Baba*, above all others. Surely, you must not forget the fine poem he wrote about you. Yes, you were his "ace Individual." You know how small boys are, Ali; about some things, they never grow up. They may hide their true feelings under pretense, but true feelings will out! You with "your precarious pills and relationships,/The loot of the sleight-of-hand,/ The sea of numbers and its froth"—Ali, Oscar really believed in you! And I think he may be the only genuine poet who ever has, or ever will.

But—perhaps Edgar Poe did—or might have—just perhaps! At least, the fancy strikes me that he would have accepted the invitation Oscar put for you.

> Let us declare a jubilee, says Ali,
> For the overplayed nervous system,
> And discuss the problems of art
> By the sterling light of the moon.

Sincerely yours,

Roy Basler

THE HEART OF BLACKNESS:
M. B. TOLSON'S POETRY

What American poet will symbolize and represent our milieu to readers in the future, as Shakespeare represents the Elizabethan Era, Milton the Puritan Era, or, to come closer home, Whitman the American Civil War Era? Will it be Eliot? Pound? Sandburg? Frost? William Carlos Williams? Time may tell, in fact is already telling, that although each of these spoke to and about us in his special voice, none of them perhaps got really to the core of us or knew us in our latitudinal-longitudinal complexity, or used quite our *whole* language with the love and imagination of a master. Will it be one of the younger generation of Roberts—Lowell, Duncan, Creeley, or—? I think not.

Even in our current dither about ecology, Eliot's *The Waste Land* seems, to me at least, something less than symbolic or representative of our age. Better than any other poem perhaps, it does convey the spiritual vacuum and intellectual wan hope that partly characterized what some view as the fading of "the Christian Era." Pound's *Cantos,* however brilliantly they project the intellectual disillusion and esthetic discord of a civilization gone rationally mad, are at best a schizoid satire, to be read obliquely. Sandburg's *The People Yes,* like all his poetic work, so subtly musical and complex in the autochthonous pagan mysticism with which it conveys the evanescence and fluidity of hard "reality," to me appears an inadequate reflection of the mind or the spirit of the age. And so on.

In thus dropping, one by one, these great contemporaries, I must admit that I am somewhat conditioned by a view of American tradition and history which the cynical may hold to be merely a vestige of our eighteenth century origins—what the historian Henry Commager has characterized as Thomas Jefferson's "prospective," as opposed to John Adams' "retrospective," concept of history and culture. With this confessed bias in mind, the reader may consider what follows, and its implications for literary study.

I suppose even those who read a great deal of modern poetry are inadequately prepared for reading a truly great poem for the first time. One's first reaction must be put off. Let's be careful, *nil admirari* as Cicero said, even when the poem comes most highly "introduced" by a scholar-poet-critic whom one respects, Allen Tate. Such was my reaction to M. B. Tolson's *Libretto for the Republic of Liberia* in 1953. Since then, things have been happening on the literary scene which make appreciation of poetry even more of a self-conscious quiddity. Remembering how M. Carl Holman's autobiographical, "The Afternoon of a Young Poet" recorded his suspicion that the white audience gave "the dancing bear. . . higher marks than a man might get for the same performance," my WASP appreciation of Tolson has had to survive some peculiar inner resistances to its own convictions, which a black critic may find it difficult to comprehend. Yet one must face the fact that literary study today is affected willy-nilly by the racial febricity in our sick society, whose antibodies seem hopefully to be overcoming the toxins, even those infecting the literary establishment.

My "appreciation," however, refuses to be squelched by the possibilities of either exaggeration or mitigation, in the view that Tolson is perhaps the poet of our era who best represents, or comes nearest to representing, in his comprehensive humanity, the broadest expanse of the American character, phrased in the richest poetic idiom of our time. Better than his contemporary peers, at their latitudinal and longitudinal extremes, he knew the span from low-brow to high-brow in both life and literature, and he loved the American English language, from gutter to ivory tower, more intimately than any of them. His poetic diction is a natural blend of home words and hall words where *hearth* and *bema* sing side by side. He is the natural poet who cultivated his nature, both root and branch, for the flower and the seed, for it was the seed even more than the flower, Ruskin to the contrary, that Tolson the poet believed art grew for—yes, the "yellow wasps of the sun swarm down," but when Tolson's "New Negro" speaks for "his America," the word is more American perhaps than any of his great contemporaries have spoken.

In his first book, *Rendezvous with America* (1944), Tolson established in his lyric strength and a relatively simple but frequently incisive diction. Most simply put his message reads:

> A man
> Is what
> He saves
> From rot.*

The success of Tolson's metaphor is its appropriateness to the poem in which it grows. In a simple poem about a great teacher whose community "struck him down" it is "the gallows of ignorance that hanged the little town." One of his best early poems, "The Ballad of the Rattlesnake," apparently the only ballad he ever wrote, epitomizes with simplicity the brutal tragedy of the sharecropper's lot, whether black or white, in the image of an Apache Indian mode of torturing a prisoner:

> The desert holds
> In its frying pan
> The bones of a snake
> And the bones of a man.
>
> And many a thing
> With a rock on its tail

---

* Quotations from *Rendezvous with America* are by permission of Dodd, Mead & Co.

Kills the nearest thing
And dies by the trail.

On the other hand, in one of his most complex and allusive later poems—more allusive even than Eliot or Pound or Hart Crane—he begins in sarcastic good humor at the expense of learning and poetry, with a metaphor that only a great poet with a great sense of humor could devise to laugh off the pomp of his proud occasion as Poet Laureate of Liberia, and follows it immediately and miraculously with magical reversal of image to exalt the living truth which escapes not only his occasion, but all occasions, and all words.

> Liberia?
> No micro-footnote in a bunioned book
>   Homed by a pedant
>   With a gelded look:
>   You are
>   The ladder of survival dawn men saw
>   In the quicksilver sparrow that slips
>   The eagle's claw!*

Reading the author's footnotes to such a marvelously complex poetic tapestry as the *Libretto for the Republic of Liberia* (1953) is almost as much of a literary adventure as reading the poem, and the impulse to add notes of one's own for their own sake is all but irresistible, in spite of the poet's serio-comic warning in the opening lines just quoted. How humorously serious in poetics this heroic ode waxes in its flamboyance seems to have escaped even the admiration in which Allen Tate wrote his introduction. Perhaps Tate did not approve Tolson's laughing about a technique Tate's masters Eliot and Pound had created all too seriously as the hallmark of modern poetry. To appreciate fully Tolson's esthetic one must abandon the humorless restraints of the "new criticism" and revel in the sheer delight of a superbly scholarly Negro artist at work with words, on a

---

* Quotations from *Libretto for the Republic of Liberia* and *The Harlem Gallery* are by permission of Twayne Publishers, Inc.

rostrum and with a message, more exalted than any ever afforded even James Weldon Johnson's preacher. No other American — one almost said no other poet — has ever blended the comic and heroic as well as the comic and tragic in a flight so high. Perhaps only a scholar-poet of a downtrodden race could have dared it. In any event, the only "creation" I have ever heard or read that even suggests viable comparison was the sermon of a well-educated Negro "holiness" preacher, many years ago, delivered to a black congregation, black except for two white college students who had slipped in and whose presence in no way inhibited, but I am inclined to think may even have further inspired, the improvisation of extempore poetry distilled by an American Negro's imagination from Hebrew sources that were our common cultural heritage. Who's afraid of big words, arcane words, low-down words, any words of any kind that are possible to poetry? Not M. B. Tolson, when he sings the meaning of *Liberia* and the hope of humanity.

The *Libretto for the Republic of Liberia* is not only one of the great odes in the English language, it is in many respects one of the finest poems of any kind published in the English language during the twentieth century, so far as my acquaintance goes. Allen Tate's minor caveats are meaningless to me in the presence of Tolson's afflatus and Jovian humor. I get carried away! And the "irony," which Tate comments on, that an American government has never, could never have, commissioned such an official poem to be read in Washington, only reminds me that I agree with Tolson that "these truths" of which Jefferson wrote, are bearing and will bear fruits for which white Americans must yet acquire the taste. Imagine if you can the humor of this black Pindar of a Mark Twain celebrating the dignity of the small African republic founded by American exslaves, with a poem at once so everyday American and yet so arcane, abstruse, and allusive that even with the author's notes it flies largely over the highbrow heads, not merely in his Liberian audience but of his fellow countrymen, white or black, literati suckled on Eliot and Pound for a quarter century! To imagine one of the less difficult but enormously pregnant passages marching across the years with heavy tread, is to appreciate

what Tolson will be when his black and white kinfolk come up to
him:

> Like some gray ghoul from Alcatraz,
> old Profit, the bald rake *paseq*, wipes the bar,
> polishes the goblet vanity,
> leers at the tigress Avarice
> as
> she harlots roues from afar:
> swallowtails unsaved by loincloths,
> famed enterprises prophesying war,
> hearts of rags *(Hanorish tharah sharinas)* souls of chalk
> laureates with sugary grace in zinc buckets of verse,
> myths rattled by the blueprint's talk,
> ists potted and pitted by a feast,
> Red Ruin's skeleton horsemen, four abreast
> . . .galloping. . .
> Marx, the exalter, would not know his East
> . . .galloping. . .
> Nor Christ, the Leveler, His West.

For one who cut his literary eyeteeth explicating the civilized
soul of T. S. Eliot's eunuch Prufrock, not to mention assorted
passages depicting psychotic brunettes fiddling "whisper music"
on their long black hair, *et cetera, et cetera,* this kind of poetry is
"a fun thing," as the collegians like to describe their own "bag"
today. Half a page of poetry with half a page of notes to explain
it, notes which themselves frequently challenge the reader no
less than does the poetry. And all for the fun of it. For example,
here is Tolson's note on the line "old Profit, the bald rake *paseq*,
wipes the bar."

> *Paseq:* "divider." This is the vertical line that occurs about 480
> times in our Hebrew Bible. Although first mentioned in the
> *Midrash Rabba* in the eleventh century, it is still the most
> mysterious sign in the literature.

How abstrusely appropriate a "visual" word can a poet find to
name his personification of the motive most extolled in the
gospel of capitalism by Chamber of Commerce evangelists? Not

merely as a "vertical" dispenser of intoxicants to the habitues of this whore house, but also, something Tolson's note does not tell us, the not-at-all mysterious use of the *paseq* in the Hebrew Bible, namely to call the tune, so that the reader will not read two words together that should properly stand apart.

What Tolson undertook, I think with great success, was to liberate the allusive, scholarly poetry Eliot created from the service of Eliot's sterile tradition and philosophy. While embelishing it with large humor, he put it to use as a vehicle for his own "prospective" view of human history.

Such is the fantastic poem published in 1953 by the poet who in 1962 was not invited to participate in "the National Poetry Festival" held at the Library of Congress, along with some thirty established poets, because he was not well enough known among the literati who had adulated Eliot and Pound for a generation. One wonders, was it the music or the theme of Tolson's song that put them off?

Anecdote of a committee. "What about Tolson?" "Who?" "M.B. Tolson, you know — *Libretto for the Republic of Liberia.*" "Oh, well, Langston Hughes and Gwendolyn Brooks are much better established."

That the committee was all white was not the trouble, for even if it had been a committee of all black poets the verdict would probably have been the same, for " 't is true 't is pity/ And pity 't is 't is true" that even yet black studies scholars seem not much better acquainted with Tolson's work than are the white scholars across the hall from them. One of our most distinguished black men of letters told me recently of reviewing for a leading publisher the manuscript of an anthology of the allegedly "best" Negro writers, which omitted M.B. Tolson but gave considerable space to Leroi Jones. It is indeed time, not only to begin revising the curricula of our schools so that the black man's contribution to American civilization may be honestly appreciated, but also to begin improving the literary judgment of the people who are revising the curricula.

It has been said by recent black writers that the black writer today must write primarily for black readers. It has also been said that the black writer must also write for white readers, or have few readers. Tolson recognized in his blood and bones as well as in his head that such statements are partial truths, and he set about writing for any reader who would take as much trouble to enjoy the reading, as he took to enjoy the writing, of poetry. Karl Shapiro has said that Tolson "writes Negro." True perhaps to some extent, but what does it mean when Tolson sounds to me more like Tolson (as Whitman sounds like Whitman) than he sounds like a Negro, and more like a man than a member of any race? It happens he was Negro-Irish-Cherokee, with as much or little as any of us to be proud of in the matter of ancestry. And intellectually he was more of the basic Jeffersonian tradition than most white Americans have ever been since Jefferson himself. For he believed in equality of "the man inside," which is the title of his tribute to his friendship with a white writer, V. F. Calverton:

> They told me—the voices of hates in the land—
> They told me that White is White and Black is Black;
> That the children of Africa are scarred with a brand
> Ineradicable as the spots on the leopard's back.
>
> They told me that gulfs unbridgeable lie
> In the no man's seascapes of unlike hues,
> As wide as the vertical of earth and sky,
> As ancient as the grief in the seagull's news.
>
> They told me that Black is an isle with a ban
> Beyond the pilgrim's Continent of Man.
>
> I yearned for the mainland where my brothers live.
> The cancerous isolation behind, I swam
> Into the deeps, a naked fugitive,
> Defying tribal fetishes that maim and damn.
>
> And when the typhoon of jeers smote me and hope
> Died like a burnt-out world and on the shore
> The hates beat savage breasts, you threw the rope
> And drew me into the catholic Evermore.
>
> We stood on common ground, in transfiguring light,
> Where the man inside is neither Black nor White.

Typical of the young black intellectuals today espousing a "Black Aesthetic" is the critic Don Lee, who in a review of Robert Hayden's *Kaleidescope*, an anthology of Afro-American poetry, dismisses Tolson because of "his capacity to lose the people that may read him," namely, the black reader. It is Lee's belief that "Afro-Americans are better prepared to pass judgment" on black writers than are white critics. The shibboleth on which black esthetes are choking is "relevance." If Tolson is not "relevant," it is because his reader, black or white, has not measured intelligence with him. Where black phrase-makers of the last instant are telling both black and white people that "violence is as American as cherry pie," Tolson would still remind us that

> . . . on the Courthouse Square
> A statue of the Lost Cause bayonets
> Contemporary air.

And, he hoped, black or white may be wise and kind as well as beautiful:

> Time
> Speaks in pantomime
> In spite of mimic clocks
> And dirty voices on the soapless box.
> Time
> Saints the unity of blood and clime
> Martyred by Caesars of the Undersoul
> Who rape the freedoms and their crimes extoll.

It is such wisdom and kindness that Tolson, somewhat atypically among midcentury black intellectuals, recognized as the essence of Abraham Lincoln's humanity. His appreciation of Lincoln as a man, attested in a remarkable piece published in the column *Caviar and Cabbage* which Tolson contributed during 1938 to the *Washington Tribune,* was further evidenced in his long poem "Abraham Lincoln of Rock Spring Farm," published in Herbert Hill's anthology *Soon, One Morning* (1963). In my judgment, this is one of the finest poems written about Lincoln since Whitman, and certainly the outstanding poem about Lincoln's genesis. It is, however, a deliberately plain, if heroic, poem, where the *Libretto* is a polyphonic and syncopated fugue. Perhaps his recognition of a certain kinship of spirit, as well as his respect for Lincoln's genius, ran close to the river bed of Tolson's frequently turbulent current of words.

Tolson's unfinished masterpiece was planned to be a major epical work, of which only the prologue, "Book I; The Curator" was published in 1965 as *The Harlem Gallery*, the year before his death, with a brilliant introduction by Karl Shapiro. Although one can only speculate about the overall plan, which called for four books—Egypt Land, The Red Sea, The Wilderness, and The Promised Land—to follow Book I: The Curator, the latter stands alone as a unique work for which traditional poetic terminology has no entirely adequate word. It is not an ode, as was the *Libretto*, though in some respects like it, but rather a kind of lyric-dramatic narrative sermon in verse. In any event, it is as carefully, and often as intricately, structured as a Tantric mandala, but swinging with Harlem rhythm and sublimely mingling the idiom of bedroom, street slang, scholarly diction, Shakespearean metaphor and foreign tongues with a controlled abandon that only a poet who had observed all levels of life and touched all aspects of language could command.

Perhaps the one other fine poem with which *The Harlem Gallery* may be compared best is Langston Hughes' *Montage of a Dream Deferred*. Both poems are deeply moving and highly charged with emotion for any reader whose humanity spans more than one extreme of the color spectrum. Both poems are distillations of American English, but Hughes writes quite legitimately as a folk poet, with no particular obeisance to or love for either the matter or the manner of literary tradition, whereas Tolson employs very nearly the entire art and learning of the Hebraic-Christian-Classical tradition, and Oriental and African literary lore as well. Comparing Hughes and Tolson, however, is like comparing Robert Burns and John Milton, either useful or useless, depending on whether one really knows both—and the difference.

Consider as illustration the section "Theta," which states

Tolson's esthetic in richly allusive, but colloquial, fashion, and clinches the bitter truth of Art from Harlem to Paris, or Rome—that pleasure and happiness are not one and the same:

No guinea pig of a spouse
to be cuckolded in a mood indigo,
no gilded in-and-out beau
to crackle a *jeu de mots* about the house —
Art, the woman Pleasure, makes no blind dates,
but keeps the end of the tryst with one:
she is a distant cousin of aeried Happiness
the lovebird seeks against the eye-wrying sun,
in spite of her fame,
dubious as Galen's sight
of a human body dissected,
in spite of the *hap* in her name,
ominous as a red light.

The claw-thrust
of a rutting tigress,
the must
of a rogue elephant —
these con the bull of predictability,
like Happiness
a capriccio bastard-daughter of Tyche.

KKK, the beatnik guitarist, used to say
to High Yellah Baby
(before he decided to rub
out the light of his eyes
in the alley of Hinnom behind the Haw-Haw Club):
"The *belle dame* — Happiness — the goofy dream of
is a bitch who plays with crooked dice
the game of love."

It is not *The Waste Land* or *The Four Quartets*, I think, which limn the present or light the future with the past so well that scholars salvaging libraries of this era may someday guess what manner of men were we. Nor is it even Sandburg's *The People, Yes*, nor William Carlos Williams' *Paterson*, but rather Tolson's

The Harlem Gallery, where the heart of blackness with the heart of whiteness lies revealed. Man, *what* do you think you are is not the white man's question but the black man's rhetorical answer to the white man's question. No poet in the English language, I think, has brought larger scope of mind to greater depth of heart than Melvin Tolson in his unfinished song to the soul of humanity.

Tolson's learning makes a mockery of the proud ignorance of a John C. Calhoun, who was quoted that "if he could find a Negro who knew Greek syntax, he would believe that the Negro was a human being." What it makes of the utterances of some of Calhoun's latter day disciples is difficult to choose a word for. But more than his learning and intelligence, it is his art that makes a mockery of all racial pride or prejudice.

The message of *The Harlem Gallery* is that art, like humanity, knows no single race or peculiar color of its own. Art is human rather than Negro, Caucasian, or whatever, and the terms African art, or European art, or Afro-American art are named for the artist's immediate audience, not for his craft or his imagination, each of which is his and not his country's or his people's, except by his largesse. So "English poetry" is a meaningless term except as it means "in English language," but "Shakespeare's poetry" or "Keats' poetry" means, as "Homer's poetry" or "Tolson's poetry," the unmistakable creation of its maker. This is a lesson that the study of any artist will teach, but that Tolson can teach with especial power, today and tomorrow.

And yet, granting the unique stamp of the creator on his matter, there is also the indubitable representation of his milieu, with which his culture has outfitted him, no less than the snake's, or the fawn's, "nature" has outfitted him, so that he "belongs." Only the intellectually and culturally deprived, especially those unaware of their deprivation, can any longer fail to see that American culture, as Albert Murray has pointed out in *The Omni-Americans*, is neither white nor black, but mulatto. And what is true of American culture in general is particularly true of American language, and is becoming more and more true of American literature. However Eliotic the retrospective tradi-

tion may seem to those who understand only what they have
been taught, the Tolsonian prospect lies certainly, and I think
clearly, ahead.

Poetry provided for M. B. Tolson what research, teaching,
writing and publication failed to provide for his black counterparts in the world of science, education, and learning — an opportunity to employ his intellect and project his identity as a
man in a realm where skin color was nonsignificant. Classical
scholarship of the highest order might not permit William S.
Scarborough to move and mingle on the level of his peers in
WASP universities or learned societies any more than historical scholarship would permit Carter G. Woodson, or scientific discovery and accomplishment would permit William A.
Hinton to receive the respect and rewards that would have been
showered upon a white man with their respective accomplishments; but classical and historical scholarship of high order, accompanied by anthropological knowledge of wide expanse, could
blend with the art of poetry to transcend the intellectual, scientific, and religious poverty of human relationships in a society
and a culture still bound by a myth of white superiority. One
might find himself forced to be a Negro historian, but not a
Negro poet. One could be a man, and proudly a Negro, and especially a poet, without specializing in being primarily the Negro
on the one hand, nor apologizing for being one on the other. This
M. B. Tolson felt, believed, declared, and demonstrated. To my
mind, this is a supreme accomplishment of an individual human
spirit in America in our day, to which moon-walking as the
supreme collective accomplishment of our engineering know-how
shines like a candle in broad daylight. Tolson refused the fate of
what he termed

> the white and not-white dichotomy
> the Afroamerican dilemma in the Arts —
> the dialectic of
> to be or not to be
> a Negro

Art was the means by which he believed not only an individual poet, but also mankind, could transcend, in some measure,

both the past and the present in the future, if mankind put art to its highest use in recreating human life. So his prospective view, like Jefferson's, saw the imagined passing into the real, rather than the reverse, as taught by a sterile school of letters, that art merely imitates. And he addressed his concluding question and answer in *The Harlem Gallery* thus:

> White Boy
> Black Boy,
> What if this Harlem Exhibition becomes
> a *cause celebre*? . . . .
>
> . . . .
> Our public may possess in Art
> a Mantegna figure's arctic rigidity;
> yet — I hazard — yet,
> this allegro of the Harlem Gallery
> is not a chippy fire,
> for here, in focus, are paintings that chronicle
> a people's New World odyssey
> from chattel to Esquire!

Tolson has written of American life as it is, and will be. He has taken our white-black culture and imagined it into a new thing more representative of the modern human condition than any of his contemporary peers among poets has managed to create, and it is not "negritude," although he has plenty of that, but "humanitude" that enabled him to accomplish the feat. I do not expect anyone to accept this judgment until he has read and appreciated Tolson's poetry for himself, and I do not expect professors of American literature to accept it generally for perhaps a quarter century, but Tolson's recognition will come as surely as has Whitman's.

A LITERARY ENTHUSIASM; OR, THE USER USED

By way of introduction and explanation of the title of this paper, I suppose it would be apropos for me to admit at this point that perhaps my greatest literary enthusiasm as a teacher of American literature for many years, was Ralph Waldo Emerson's Yankee prose, and most particularly his Phi Beta Kappa address, "The American Scholar." Whatever literary or scholarly enthusiasm I can still muster has been greatly stimulated by a rereading of that noble address, and relating it to the living evidence that the Emersonian gospel is still given something more than lip service by at least a segment of our academic community.

Everyone—male, female, or in-between—wakes up to the fact, at some stage of understanding, that one is being used, by others, for their own purposes. This is seldom a welcome discovery, whether the *user* is a parent or a sibling or some more distant relation, even to the remotest branches of the family of man—or, for that matter of nature (who, for example, has remained unaware that he is being used by the family pet, cat or

This essay was originally delivered as the Phi Beta Kappa Address at the College of William and Mary, 5 December 1969.

dog, or by the glossy patented rose he cultivates with care?). Whoever he is, the *used* is likely to resent the fact at some point in his experience and rebel against it.

The baby on occasion refuses to nurse. Who wants to be a daily disposal device for milk, of all things?

The child threatens to run away, and sometimes does. Who wants to be the possessed object of either parental pride or parental disgust, reward or discipline? And it is not only the Portnoys who complain, either. The adult goes on a binge, takes a trip, or takes revenge, violent or subtle. Who wants to let his user get off scot-free?

Of course, it is preferable to be the *user* rather than the *used*, or so it would seem. This illusion may be mutual. Observe the radiant angelism of the contented suckling at the teat, or that of the contented suckler on the other side of the activity, at least until the operation reaches the point where the satiated suckling bites, just for fun, and gets smacked for his pains. Perhaps this is the first rude awakening on the infant's part, one hopes not on the mother's part, although too often mothers (and fathers) seem never to become fully aware that the parent-child relationship can only be moderately successful at best, when the parent (and by the parent's example, it may be hoped, eventually the child) keeps constantly, if warily, before him, the mutual illusion of a *summum bonum* of *user* as *used*.

I have said "so it would seem" to modify my observation that it is preferable to be *user* rather than *used*. Still, there should be some sophistication about this common illusion. But keeping Emerson in mind here too, the question is what kind of sophistication?

One must be very hard-boiled, perhaps, but not like Ernest Hemingway, or perhaps very soft-boiled, but not like Marilyn Monroe. In either case, to live for years on the assumption that the world is one's oyster, and then wake up one morning, or go to bed one night, choking on it, can only bring the remedy of a shotgun blast or alcohol lethally laced with Seconal. What is even more tragic, or would be, were it not merely pathetic at this late date in human history, is for the greediest and craftiest of users to become aware, too late, that he (or she) has been used —

and how! — all along, while under a persistent infantile illusion
that one was really using rather than being used. Think of us
modern sybarites who can't stop gorging and suffocating on the
good things of our civilization because we have to support the
way of life our commerce and industry are making obligatory —
three cars in every garage (each with its lethal exhaust pipe)
because what's good for General Motors is good for us. Pity the
pathetic *used* executive with his ulcer. I'd like to try his ulcer if I
could get his house along with it, thinks the ghetto boy.

But let me extrapolate a little, since all my scientifically
mathematical, biological, psychological, and sociological colleagues do it, and it's "the thing." If I can judge from what I
read, the great personal problem of our day is sex. I've been
reading a lot of sex novels lately — in fact it is hard to find anything else in the way of new fiction. The day when Dreiser's
Genius did something else, at least during the day time, has
given way to the day and night when Philip Roth's *Portnoy* or
Ivan Gold's *Sick Friends* simply gabble between copulations,
straight and oblique, or/and masturbation, with or without
some assisting fetish or stimulant, or both, to send them off. And
while we don't have to read them any more than we have to buy
General Motors' cars (there's always *Henry Esmond* or *David
Copperfield)*, what's good for Grove Press seems to be in a fair
way of becoming like what's good for General Motors, and
therefore good for us.

But that's not precisely where I want my first extrapolation to
take me. I want to move rather to the sad recognition scene in
the typical modern novel, the scene where the hero or heroine
discovers what he or she should have known all along — at least
the reader knew it — namely, that either, or each, has been *had*,
when both thought they were *having* — the *user* as *used*. Whereupon the hero or heroine becomes "turned off" as current slang
puts it (temporarily, of course, or there would be no modern fiction), turned off forsooth because he or she discovers that the
objective correlative, to be strictly literary about the problem,
doesn't after all correlate. The subjective, poetic, infantile fantasy of sexual gratification has proved a dream or a myth, albeit
renewable, as any good life insurance policy should be. It's

enough to make a philosopher or a naturalist, or a natural philosopher, weep genuine crocodile tears.

Of course, both naturalists and philosophers recognized long before our scientific age that nature invented sex for other ends than (or at least *as well as*) ours. And that the exquisite pleasure was to insure life, not to indulge it. People have been trying for a long time, with too little success, alas, to circumvent nature biologically. But perhaps the most successful effort at circumvention of biological sex has still been primarily psychological — homosexuality being the most effective deterrent to the population explosion. The basic fact of human sexuality has proved to be not biological but psychological, and as such practically uncircumventable. The only way to have your cake and eat it too is to make a trade with someone else. All of the dream work, idealism, or what-have-you of sickness or sainthood, from the hippie song in *Hair* "masturbation can be fun," to *Portnoy's Complaint,* cannot make persistent autoeroticism into a fun thing, because it is not only not intercourse, it is not even self-knowledge. Although laboratory prophets have been warning us that the twentieth century may be the last in which the sexual act is a desirable, if not really necessary, condition for human reproduction, I for one cannot conceive of the time when it will become psychologically, if not spiritually (to use an old-fashioned word) unrewarding, Masters and Johnson to the contrary, notwithstanding.[1]

Now for my real extrapolation. I intend to try to apply this theme to the intellectual community as represented by our colleges and universities, the social community as represented by the WASP establishment, and the politico-economic community as represented right now by you know who. And that's "about as far as you can go," as the fellow said in Oscar Hammerstein's song, "Everything's Up-to-date in Kansas City."

College students today seem to have awakened to the fact that they are being used to perpetuate an intellectual community and a socioeconomic establishment that has its own selfish interest

---

[1] Since this was written Masters and Johnson have reported a new study which substantiates "scientifically" my precise point.

at heart more than theirs. Whatever this individual variety of revolt — new left, black militant, or drug-oriented flower children — they all agree that they won't be used by an establishment which seems to them hypocritical, not to say dishonest, in its use of human beings in general, and of young people in particular. Whatever the establishment has been telling itself about what is good for us professors, us parents, us politicians, us whatever, being therefore good for young people too, a considerable number of young people refuse any longer to accept. This is not entirely a new thing, of course; it was true to some extent in my student days, but with some difference. We knew we could always leave home or quit school, and our elders could make it very plain that they would say "Good riddance — if you want to run things your own way, then find someplace else to do it." Many did, and woke up to the fact that they were still being used, by somebody else than their parents or teachers, as they began to make their own way, using others on their own part, as they went.

Today this is no longer possible, or at least not to the extent that it once was. Parents cannot tell their teen-age Dharma bums and hippies to get out and make their own way if they don't like the rules of the family establishment. Kids can "drop out" or "cop out," but not *usefully*. A youngster under sixteen can't legally hold a job on his own responsibility, even as a migrant worker or field hand, as he could when I was under sixteen. (He can't, that is, unless accompanied by his parents, equally exploited along with him.) He can't bum his way to the Kansas wheat fields in summer, or work on a freighter, or do much of anything on his own. It was not that most of us did such things, but we could, and some few of us did if we were rebellious enough to want to take the consequences. I can't speak too well for the girls of my generation, but I knew quite a number of nice ones who took off at a pretty early age into a labor force that exploited them to the utmost. But they escaped their parental exploitation, or community, or school, or whatever they thought they were escaping—out of the frying pan and into the fire.

Of course, we were being used by the establishment then, even when we had our illusion of freedom. The establishment uses everybody, and always has, and the smart ones are allegedly those who find out their own way of making the operation as mutual as possible, to their own advantage, but the even smarter ones perhaps are those who get together to change the establishment to suit them better.

One difference between my day as a young person and the present is that our young ones today have had their individual rebellions pressed into cohesive group movements to some extent by the paradoxical combination of an increasingly comprehensive and rigid establishment on one hand and an increasingly permissive (amoral if not immoral) and rational nonethic, on the other hand. Authority, parental or governmental, has come to seem so grossly and merely a matter of possessive exploitation or physical power, with no satisfactory moral or spiritual justification undergirding it, that escape by drugs or rebellion by confrontation is attracting more and more of the so-called "best minds" of our younger generation every day. Neither law nor order, promulgated by apparently hypocritical, self-serving, establishmentarian politics, adjudicated by apparently hypocritical, self-serving, establishmentarian courts, and enforced by police whose uniforms have become a symbol of mere force to a growing segment of our young people, — neither law nor order, it seems, represents anything more than the means by which the establishment enforces its ultimate use of the *used* on the *used*, whether they like it or not. Some of them are talking about it as the modern version of slavery.

If the establishment looks this way to more and more of the supposedly "Best minds," how does it look to the intellectually less well endowed? It would seem to look the same, only more so, if one may judge by what is being reported from our city streets and rural lanes. And one begins to wonder, what one could not have wondered even a decade ago, whether a new, wholly different kind of revolution than the world has ever seen before, might be upon us in the not distant future. The *used* know that they cannot be dispensed with and are telling us that they will be full partners and help make some new rules of the game. Now, what does the establishment do under the circumstances? Persuade them to keep their place? Force them to keep their place? Send them to concentration camps? Some authoritarian voices in the land would seem to believe this can be done. Or shall we try to take them into the establishment to some extent on their own terms, revising the laws (about drug use, for instance) and rules (of sexual relations, for example), putting them on boards and other policy-setting bodies (to make curricula or community programs for instance), but above all, making them full citizens at least by age eighteen, with the right to vote as well as fight and die in a war they never made and don't want. Let's remember that the attainment of one's majority at twenty-one years was legally defined by an exploitative society, to retain the child's *use* for the father, or under apprenticeship, the master, and is long since obsolete, especially for purposes of citizenship in a democracy. Why shouldn't one vote even at sixteen years of age?

What do we do? The fact that Dr. Milton Eisenhower's commission report has made such recommendations does not make me particularly happy, for everything that report recommends has been recommended by intelligent people for years, and ignored by the establishment with its customary self-serving hypocrisy. The establishment seems to have as much difficulty today as it did in 1860 or 1776, to name only two of many relevant dates, in recognizing that it is not really the acme of civilization, after all, but at best merely a viable and pliable stage in an evolutionary development, or at worst an obsolete and ossified form ripe for revolutionary destruction in order that renascence may take place. If it *is* the latter, neither our government nor our society is at fault, but we ourselves. As Emerson reminded his age, "Every law and usage was a man's expedient to meet a particular case. . . . We may make as good, we may make better."

Although obfuscated by centuries of cant, hypocrisy, and self-righteousness, the situation is really simple: (1) people can't make out very well without each other; (2) no individual likes to be used on terms he has not agreed to; (3) a two-way communication is necessary to any mutual relationship. As a young radical put it to me "our professors are engaging, for the most part, in intellectual masturbation, for they certainly aren't having intellectual intercourse with us!"

There seems to me to be no real possibility but to make some changes. We are long overdue, I agree, to create a more meaningful role not merely for college undergraduates but for high school teenagers and even younger children. In the same way that the establishment has depersonalized us into "teachers," "consumers," "lawyers," or whatnot, it has depersonalized them into "students," or "adolescents." Going to school or playing games is not enough for either the brilliant or the more modestly endowed. We are long overdue to create a more meaningful role for black people in general and for young black people in particular. Young blacks, as well as young whites, are simply not going to be used in the future as they have been in the past, and if I am any judge of what is happening, young whites and blacks are more and more joining forces against the establishment for the first time in our history.

The only thing that has ever really distinguished the United States of America is an idea phrased, if not actually invented, by Thomas Jefferson. In Abraham Lincoln's day, the question was whether the Jeffersonian idea applied to black people, and Lincoln defined, years before the Civil War, a minimum economic application when he said of a black woman, that even if not equal in all respects, "in her natural right to eat the bread she earns with her own hands without asking leave of any one else, she is my equal, and the equal of all others." I think we all, or nearly all, admit today that Lincoln's minimum is not nearly enough, but few white people are willing to go so far as black militants seem to be demanding — an actual dividing up of the country's assets. Basically, however, it seems to me that young blacks are demanding something even more fundamental than property or money. Just like young whites, they are demanding first the right to determine for themselves the use to be made of them, and only secondarily to have a voice in the distribution of

the economic rewards for that use. In their first demand they
are joining forces with young white people in ever-increasing
numbers. Both black and white are refusing to accept the role
dictated for them by the commercial-industrial-military establishment which alleges it knows what is best.

Sometimes there seems to be a solidarity of insensitivity on
the part of the older generation, white and black alike. When
Vice-President Agnew laid the law down to his fourteen-year-old
daughter about not wearing an armband in recognition of the so-
called moratorium, and then announced his private, family
episode to the press for political purposes, he obtained plaudits
even from unexpected quarters. For example, black newspaper
columnist William Raspberry, with admonition to black parents
whose children are allegedly running wild, commented,"It would
be a mistake, of course, to try to run a country that way. But it
doesn't seem a bad way to run a family." One wonders. Isn't the
problem of running the country actually somewhat the same
problem, for which the establishment today, like Papa Agnew,
undertakes to enforce by sheer authority a highly debatable, if
not actually a hypocritical or quite possibly dishonest, position?
In any event, the parent who thus enforces his authority may
wake up to a more bitter defeat in another year or so, when his
child becomes a young adult, like many others, who despises all
the father represents. Perhaps there are some changes to be
made.

It is obvious that the young do not have all the answers,
though some of them seem to think they have them all. But they
may have some of them, and it is obvious that their parents
don't have, and never have had, all the answers themselves.
Whatever the answers turn out to be, the *used* as well as the
users will eventually have a voice.

Now I should like to return to Emerson with particular
reference to today's college and university community, which
continues to be one of the principal foci of the discontented,
where the traditional *used* and *user* relationship has been but
feebly modified as yet, for the most part with makeshift or inadequate palliatives. Having been removed for more than twenty
years from the shelter of academic life, but also having preserved continuing contact and a more than nostalgic interest, I

think I can take an understanding, if not an unbiased, view.

More than 130 years ago, Emerson undertook to describe and define the duty of the American scholar. "In the right state, he is *Man Thinking.* In the degenerate state, when the victim of society, he tends to become a mere thinker, or, still worse, the parrot of other men's thinking." In other words, he is merely the *used*, and has not waked up to the fact.

So much for Emerson. Here are two somewhat extended contemporary statements, one by a Columbia University student and the other by a professor of law at Columbia. Let us each judge for himself which of the two is more the *"Man Thinking"* of Emerson's definition. Both student and professor were commenting (*Columbia Forum*, Fall 1969) on Columbia's newly but belatedly organized senate, which has a modest representation of students along with a majority representation of faculty and a few assorted representatives of administration, trustees, and alumni. Here is the anonymous student's comment, somewhat abridged:

> The new Senate is a procedural change and not a meaningful change. It does not address itself to some of the basic questions — what is the function of a university, and what is its relationship to society, and its responsibility to the community.
>
> There is no question in my mind that the university is geared to preserve American capitalism, to preserve the rich and the super rich. There is fantastic waste in the United States. Not only waste of material, but waste of human life. I'm not just talking about the waste of lives in the Vietnam war; I'm talking about people's lives being wasted when all their talent, their time and energy, is devoured by American capitalism to produce products which supposedly fill people's needs, but obviously don't. Who trains people to do this? The university. This is perhaps its gravest involvement with the corporations.
>
> The university is an agent of oppression. Any talk about a university senate and committees is irrelevant and stupid. It is a form of social control, of pacification, of co-optation. It diverts energy into institutions that are not open to change.

Here is Professor Michael Sovern's comment, also somewhat abridged:

I would challenge the nonsensical argument that the university functions to support the war and oppression. It's ironic that the big bogeyman of last year was IDA [the Institute for Defense Analyses] — and IDA came out over the summer with a research document opposing the ABM. . . .

No, I see the essential function of the university as teaching and research. Restructuring will not change that. In a way, the Senate is itself a pedagogical instrument — for all its members, not just for students. If it functions well, all who participate will be able to make wiser decisions about their university. They will, however, be seeking what we have always sought at Columbia: to help the young to learn and the scholar to carry on significant research.

Which of these two, student or professor (and one of the more enlightened, at that), is more Emerson's *"Man Thinking"* and which is more Emerson's "mere thinker," repeating accepted concepts?

Now I want to make it perfectly clear, as President Nixon says, that I do not agree entirely with either student or professor, particularly about the prospects for good in Columbia's new structure for running a university, about which I certainly don't know enough. But I think I can detect the pattern which qualifies one of the two comments as more that of "man thinking" and the other as more that of a "mere thinker." For the one thing Emerson helped me to recognize many years ago — and I liked to think at the time that he accomplished it also for many of my students, at least temporarily — was an understanding of the difference. Of course, this did not solve any problem, either mine or my students', but only brought about recognition of the nature of the problem of thinking itself.

I have heard it stated with considerable pride by the dean of a leading professional school in one of our universities, that most of the student rebellion today is fomented by the more irresponsible arts and humanities students, with a sprinkling of science majors, but that, thank God, law students, medical students and engineering students are not taking part at all, having more important things to do. I suspect that the dean is less than one hundred percent right about his own students, but even so, what relevance does the alleged fact have to Emerson's definition of the scholar, as well as to the Columbia student's recognition that the modern university has become largely an establishmentarian service station? Were I a professor of American Literature today, and not entirely polarized, I should take pride, I think, in the fact that it is the liberal arts students who make up the majority of "the movement," with all their half-baked, practical idealism. They are at least men and women thinking about a world that must be changed. They seek an active redefinition of the user-used relationship, to restore the mutual illusion of "satisfaction" to its former "usefulness" in society.

At this point I shall bring my observations to an end, rather than to a conclusion, leaving us with our feet firmly planted in midair, as Emerson frequently left his audiences many years ago. I have little doubt that more persons will react to what I have been trying to set forth in much the same way that the establishmentarian Reverend John Pierce did to Emerson's address in 1837, but I cannot think of a better way to make my final point about this problem of understanding than by quoting Pierce: "Rev. Ralph Waldo Emerson gave an oration of 1¼ hour, on the American Scholar. . . . He professed to have method; but I could not trace it, except in his own annunciation."

WHO DO YOU THINK
YOU ARE?

Some years ago I was asked to lecture to a contingent of the Peace Corps on "the American character." I accepted with alacrity and then began worrying about what I could possibly say on the subject which would be of any value to my special audience. I felt no reluctance for lack of qualifications. I had read the Europeans as well as our own writers who described Americans from the eighteenth century to the present, and I had made my own observations for about half a century. I felt that perhaps I was as much of an expert on the subject as any of them. What then gave me cause for concern, and still does, was the fact that although I thought I knew the American character I did not believe it possible to describe it adequately. Human character is, and always has been, such a bundle of contradictions and ambiguities that those who have observed and written about it have been able to see in it almost anything they want to see. Furthermore, I could not honestly say that I completely understood what I knew, but then I reflected that none of the experts on the subject seemed to me to understand it any better than I.

Certainly one of the most respected and stimulating analyses made in our own day is David Riesman's *The Lonely Crowd* (1950). Riesman uses the methods that modern sociology and

psychology can bring to bear on American society and con-
cludes that whereas our ancestors were formerly tradition-
directed, and later inner-directed, contemporary Americans are
chiefly other-directed and are becoming more other-directed
every day. Although "arrived at," this conclusion remains un-
proved to my satisfaction. As I have studied Americans of the
past, both as individuals and as members of society, it has seemed
to me that their tradition-direction is so frequently indistinguishable from their other-direction, and so mixed up with their
inner-direction, in both individual and group character, whether
in New England, or South Carolina, or on the frontier, that to
assess any individual or group as being directed chiefly by tradition, other people, or inner light is a matter of informed guessing and little else. Likewise, when I try to analyze the other-
direction apparent in the people I know, it breaks down into
about equal parts of tradition-direction and inner-direction, and
the inner-direction which Riesman believes to be on the wane is
manifested on all sides by my supposedly other-directed contemporaries. The better I know the individual, the more certain I am
of his inner-direction. In fact, the very evidences of his other-
direction frequently seem to me to be dictated by the particular
inner person that he is.

The more I know about any historical individual or any historical community, the less I can see him or it fitting neatly into
Riesman's thesis. For example, Benjamin Franklin and
Abraham Lincoln. Were either of them representative of an
inner-directed age? I believe I could, if space permitted, show
many and large evidences of how powerfully other-directed each
man was and how certainly tradition-direction helped mold both
their lives in a large measure. In fact, each man candidly admitted that his principal inner-direction was his desire to be well
thought of by other people and that his actions were motivated
by this desire above all others. Yet there are no examples of
inner-directed character more cogent than the lives of these two
men, each of whom has come to be, in the round, symbolic of the
age in which he lived.

As for the societies in which our ancestors had their milieu,
whether in Puritan New England, or a southern colony like the
Oglethorpe one in Georgia, or on the western frontier, other-

direction seems to me to have been in each of them, in their respective eras, as potent a force as it is in our mechanized modern society. Inner-direction was severely circumscribed by Puritan society. Remember what happened to the Quakeress Anne Hutchinson: Her inner-direction was not tolerable to Massachusetts, and she took her persecuted family to Rhode Island. Can one imagine the average member of Jonathan Edwards' congregation relying entirely on his own conscience? Non-conformity was Emerson's doctrine in the nineteenth century, but it was certainly no more an accepted doctrine of the average American of that day than of this.

Or consider what happened to James G. Birney in the frontier community of Huntsville, Alabama, early in the nineteenth century. His inner-direction told him slavery was wrong, and he missed no opportunity to say so. As a result he was ostracized and driven out of the community by his neighbors who would tolerate no non-conformity on the question of the purportedly God-given prerogatives of slave owners.

I, for one, cannot see convincing evidence that there is any one "dominant element" in our national character in the present or the past, on a continuing day-by-day, year-by-year basis. The interplay of those motivating forces, whatever they are, which Riesman designates as "inner-direction" and "other-direction" (new names for Emersonian old friends, "self-reliance" and "conformity"—which, by the way, illustrates what sociological terminology does to philosophical and literary thought, without very much improving either our understanding of the phenomenon "character" or our interpretation of ancestors or contemporaries)—such interplay is only a seesaw on which most of us, like most of our ancestors, alternately move up and down, both as initiators and initiates in the fraternity of mankind.

Another book of the Chicago school of thought with a thesis somewhat related to Riesman's is Daniel Boorstin's *The Image; or, What Happened to the American Dream* (1962). In it the author posits that the *ideal* which motivated and inner-directed Americans in the past has been replaced by the *image*, which motivates and other-directs Americans in the present. The image, of course, is a hoax manipulated by Madison Avenue, and we are all in a fair way to becoming the phonies we are pictured as being because we have succumbed to the illusions of television, movies, and the press, and we think that it doesn't make much difference whether we are somebody or not so long as our image is satisfactorily projected. It is certainly true that the ancient Hindu concept that all things of this world are illusions has been given a new twist by modern technology, which enables "Everyman" to join the parade and then go home and see himself as a participant in history on the TV late news, but I wonder whether we are as unsophisticated philosophers as Boorstin seems to think. I doubt it. And I think Boorstin knows that his astringent thesis and the marvelous array of instances which he assembles themselves portray, as a whole, an image of America which a Russian might observe with delight but would not dare count on as a guarantee of our gullibility when the chips are down. For although we may kid ourselves, and others, we do not kid ourselves as we kid others. It seems to me that Boorstin is confusing himself by his thesis, taking the mere prevalence of a certain lingo of "images" (made into a cliché by Madison Avenue) as an evidence that human nature is changing, when it is merely idiom that is changing. Can he believe that there ever was a time when people were not concerned relatively as much as they are now with "how they appear" — their image — or when they were more concerned with "how they are" — their reality? And though he flatly states, "Images now displace ideals," he fails to document the fact to my satisfaction, with his evidence so largely drawn from promotional and advertising literature, which to my knowledge has never been the definitive repository of either the ideal or the real.

Both ideal and real are reflected honestly, not in advertising and propaganda but rather in our best writers, who are trying to say what they believe is true. It is as silly to take a modern celebrity's testimonial in a cigarette advertisement as an evidence of the image's displacement of the ideal in twentieth-century American society, as to take Abraham Lincoln's testimonial in an 1860 soap advertisement as an evidence of the image's displacement of nineteenth-century American ideals. It is amusing to know that Lincoln wrote such a testimonial, with tongue in

cheek, as follows: "Professor Gardner, Dear Sir: Some speci-
mens of your soap have been used at our house and Mrs. L.
declares it a superb article. She at the same time, protests that I
have never given sufficient attention to the 'soap question' to be
a competent judge. Yours truly, A. Lincoln." (*The Collected
Works of Abraham Lincoln*, IV, 122-123) I think all of us would
recognize that, while somewhat revealing, this is hardly the best
document in which to seek for Lincoln's ideals.

Yet I do not wish to leave the impression that I think
Boorstin's book is without value. It exposes facets of American
life that need to be exposed as indubitably phony. Our history is
largely, both past and present, the story of the individual's fight
with society, and I admire Boorstin's fight with what he
despises, even though I can't agree with his sweeping judgment
that a phony image has displaced the American dream.

In a similar vein, the British historian Arnold Toynbee in his
book *America and the World Revolution* (1962) tells us that
Americans have fallen away from the spirit of 1776 and our own
revolution, which set off the revolutionary crisis that now in-
volves the whole world, and that we now are suspicious of anything but the status quo. Two aspects of America Toynbee
emphasizes as disfigurements to the American image abroad: (1)
our affluence, and (2) race feelings. Our conspicuous wealth as a
nation and our addiction to superfluous material acquisitions is
an insult to the majority of the human race, which Toynbee
believes (I think misguidedly) cannot hope to attain the level of
consumption that Madison Avenue persuades us to achieve.
Race feeling results in our self-imposed isolation in countries
like India. But this is not all; as Toynbee describes us, we are so
crippled by our addiction to things American that the American
abroad is universally a homesick, hypercritical, unsocial animal,
unable to associate sympathetically even with people who speak
his own language.

As an American historian, Henry Steele Commager, has
observed somewhere, there is a real question whether Americans can adapt themselves to revolutions outside the United
States, insofar as they affect America. Heretofore, we have been
able to enjoy revolution and the status quo at the same time. The

crucial problem for the next generation is whether it can develop the inventiveness and resourcefulness necessary to counter the forces making for a dangerous kind of bigness and conformity in America.

A Japanese scholar, Makoto Oda, has classified Americans in two categories: "straight" and "oblique." The "straights" are the majority who glorify the United States as "God's own country"; the "obliques" have their doubts about this and are willing to compromise with other ideologies, some of them even regarding communism as not an unmitigated evil. He believes that "straight America . . . is gradually being engulfed by oblique America." ("Waga Furuburaito no nakamatachi," *Chuo Koron*, 898, August 1962, p. 158)

These are just a few of the "authorities" who have been analyzing American character in recent years. It's anybody's game and everybody's business, apparently. So I put the question to Americans and others as well.

Who do you think you are, anyway? Not long ago I heard that question on the street, as I have heard it countless times during my life, but it had never before struck me with quite the significance that it came to have in connection with my mulling over the American character.

The circumstance was that an altercation had broken out between two boys in a group of half a dozen. I do not know what the fuss was about, and the fact probably would not be important anyway. One of the boys was obviously throwing his weight around, and the other challenging him, "Who the hell do you think you are, anyway?"

The retort was as traditional as the question, as traditional as the identical question and retort were during my boyhood, nearly half a century ago. "I'll *show* you who I am, you *S-O-B!*"

I say the retort was traditional, and I believe every American has heard and probably himself shouted this same question and/or retort too many times in like circumstances not to know just how much it is a part of the American tradition. But we all know that insofar as we are tradition-directed in this, we are asserting an inner-direction which has been, is, and, I believe, will continue to be, the dominant trait of American character.

Note that I believe in *traits* not *elements of character*, not being a sociologist.

There is one fact about this instance that I have not mentioned up to this point because it stresses a belief I subscribe to as certainly as I do to anything in my American heritage. The group was made up of Negro boys and white boys, and the two who were disputing were *not* of the same color. This precise combination would scarcely have occurred during my boyhood, and the fact that it does occur more frequently today is significant of something that has happened, in the interim, to both tradition-direction and inner-direction in the darker segment of American society, which has begun to assume and demonstrate that it too is as American as "Whitey."

The quest for identity has been the theme of American literature from James Fenimore Cooper to William Faulkner. All of our great writers have told one story—of men and women seeking to learn who they are, and in the performance of the quest finding out and showing who they are—creating their identity out of the stuff of life itself. Think of Cooper's Natty Bumppo, Melville's Ishmael in *Moby Dick*, Hawthorne's Hester, Mark Twain's Huck Finn, Walt Whitman's "Myself," or Faulkner's Colonel Sutpen in *Absalom, Absalom!*, Sinclair Lewis' Carol Kennicot or Arrowsmith, or even Babbitt, who illustrate the theme in a way no less cogent because satirical. Or think of a great introspective autobiography like *The Education of Henry Adams*, or an autobiography almost devoid of introspection like Benjamin Franklin's, both alike in being the story of one man's quest for his identity and the demonstration of what each so differently created for his identity. Or read James Baldwin's deeply moving story of his own quest in *Go Tell It on the Mountain*, or his more recent *Nobody Knows My Name*.

This quest for identity begins for an American child, as for any other child, in the play and struggle of fitting himself into the environment into which he has been born, without choice on his part, with a name given by parents and a nationality given by a government, neither of which has any meaning for him except as he makes a meaning of them for himself. The novelist Ralph Ellison has dealt concretely and creatively with this theme as the clue to his growth and development as a writer, and much of what he says is true of white as well as Negro, just as it is true of people in all occupations and stations of life, as well as of writers and artists: "Our names being the gifts of others must be made our own. . . . For many of us this is far from easy. We must learn to wear our names within all the noise and confusion of the environment in which we find ourselves; make them the center of all of our associations with the world; with man and with nature. We must charge them with all our emotions, our hopes, hates, loves, aspirations. They must become our masks and our shields, and the containers of all those values and traditions which we learn and/or imagine as being the meaning of our familial past." ("Hidden Name and Complex Fate," *The Writer's Experience*, The Library of Congress, Washington, 1964, p. 3)

In American history, also, there are hundreds of examples of this quest, but there is no more dramatic example of how one man's *quest* for identity *created* identity than that afforded by the life of Abraham Lincoln. At the beginning of his career, Lincoln's first political speech announced: "Every man is said to have his peculiar ambition. Whether it be true or not, I can say for one that I have no other so great as that of being truly esteemed of my fellow men, by rendering myself worthy of their esteem. How far I shall succeed in gratifying this ambition, is yet to be developed." (*The Collected Works*, I, 8) This was in 1832. In 1865, thirty-three years later, he spoke of striving to finish the work he was in, "with firmness in the right, as God gives us to see the right." (VIII, 333) Other-directed, tradition-directed, but above all inner-directed, Lincoln created during the thirty-three intervening years an identity by which he is known throughout the world.

The history of the American nation was, as Lincoln saw it in his day, the history of a people's quest for identity and a creating of an identity not then complete. Lincoln delivered his Gettysburg Address with emphasis on the future. In our own day, we should remember Robert Frost's little poem, "The Gift Outright," recited at President Kennedy's inauguration, and the discussion apropos of a change in the wording of the last line.

Such as we were we gave ourselves outright
(The deed of gift was many deeds of war)
To the land vaguely realizing westward,
But still unstoried, artless, unenhanced,
Such as she was, such as she would become. (*A Witness Tree*,
1942, p. 41)

For the occasion, President Kennedy suggested the change of
"would become" to "will become." Frost's agreement, that the
change *might* suit the occasion, was compatible with his personal feeling that although what the United States *has become*
is no cause for hanging one's head in shame, and what she *will
become*, as a new President in the flush of victory might like to
have prophesied, also might be temporarily apropos, the continuing meaning of his poem, like the continuing meaning of the
Gettysburg Address, lies in the unchangeable questing word of
the poem Frost wrote many years ago, with no thought of any
President's inauguration.

Such as she was, such as she *would* become.

Whatever image exists of yourself cannot be made, even with
the help or hindrance of others, by anyone but you, and whatever image of America exists at any given time in history or in
the mind of any person or group of persons is, and can only be,
made by Americans. What Crèvecœur said about us in the eighteenth, or what Dickens said in the nineteenth century, or what a
perceptive Scandinavian like Sigmund Skard, or an informed
Englishman like Arnold Toynbee says about us today could be
said only because Americans are creating something which must
be talked about, described, exposited, and criticized. And what
Boorstin or Riesman presents in sociological analysis of our
society is only one modern American's analysis and interpretation of how his fellows appear to him. It is all very well for us
to try, as Robert Burns put it, to see ourselves as others see us.
But we should remember that an image is only an image. We are
the reality, and our quest for identity is still viable.

Can an American say anything about the American character
that is any more reliable than what a European or an Oriental

can say? The truth about Americans is the consistency of our contradictions. We are a practical and a materialistic people, but given to mysticism beyond measure. We are a selfish people, always interested in taking care of number one, but our largess has been demonstrated to surpass *in fact* even the richest myths of liberal giving. We are a self-reliant people, but we are so filled with self-doubt that we crave more than anything else to be understood and appreciated. We are an honest people who are shocked to discover our self-deceit, and who strive to redefine our honesty to prevent self-deception. If we are essentially different in these respects from any other people on the face of the earth, I do not know it. But I cannot speak for other peoples, as I think I can for most of us, when I say that Americans have fostered and even exaggerated the efficacy of self-criticism as our chief means to the end of improvement. In the home, in the church, in the school, we have learned that the only reliable measure of our success is our own failure, rather than another man's success or failure. As a nation, likewise, we have from the beginning had to measure the successes of our experiment in government largely by its failures rather than by the comparative failure or success of other systems. Much of the seemingly deep pessimism and bitter criticism of American life that characterizes our best writers is an expression of this spirit. But the curious thing about this seeming pessimism is that most of it is the self-analysis of a character that says *yea* rather than *nay* to experience, be it ever so dirty, bitter, stupid, vain, or cruel—for example, Twain or Faulkner. On the other hand, there is the American booster who seems to want everyone to admire whatever it is he is trying to sell, whether soap flakes or "a beautiful way of life." It is because he is so successful at his trade that he has come to be taken for the typical American, when he is only the most obvious American.

There is one thing, however by which the American people are identified, given credit and blame throughout the world, and which has been recognized increasingly, for more than a century, as the dominant unpleasant trait of American society, attributable to American character. This is the roughshod march of scientific and technological revolution which is rapidly destroying the traditional simplicities of life in every country in the world. The tensions in modern society are everywhere unpleasant, not only to the American beatnik poet who howls about them but also to the American organization man who tries to keep his sanity as well as his job, and to Everyman, who tries to keep up with the hectic pace dictated by "things" that seem to be in the saddle and riding mankind, as Emerson phrased it more than a century ago. This is fundamentally what Americanization means to the rest of the world. Superficially it may mean juke-box jazz or the epics of violence that American movies carry abroad—two efflorescences of technology which, like it or not, represent us more often than the Declaration of Independence, the Gettysburg Address, or all our foreign-aid programs put together. Whether a relatively sophisticated citizen of western Europe who dislikes the encroachment of Coca-Cola and the atom bomb on his sense of security, or a devout tribal African who resists the idea that his ancestral verities are just so much superstition to be jettisoned in order to become a civilized citizen of the twentieth century, the man who detests pressure has come to identify the source of pressure with Americans and Americanization, and to blame us rather than the scientific and technological revolution as the cause of his insecurity, his disillusion, his tension, and his own inadequacy to resist the trend. John Osborne's central character in *Look Back in Anger* puts this feeling succinctly in the remark, "It's pretty dreary living in the American age, unless you are an American, of course." (p. 17)

America has become the cultural pressure center in the twentieth century that western Europe was in the eighteenth and nineteenth, and now even the western European resents what we are doing to him, just as the Oriental resented and still resents what western Europeans did to him a century ago. The fine distinctions that can be drawn between "now" and "then" are of little solace to the man who feels that he is being pushed around. We should understand this and try to do what we can to alleviate the resentment, but more important for us is the necessity of learning to accept the responsibility, take the blame no less than the credit, for what we show and do to the rest of·the world as well as to ourselves.

While I do not want to minimize the strong and sometimes desirable resistance to change which is and always has been present in the American character, I believe that the American people have demonstrated their especial dedication to the principle that society and the individual must develop and use the discoveries and inventions of the human mind. By discoveries and inventions, I do not mean merely machines and gadgets but also the ideas which are revolutionizing our understanding of nature and human nature. Our dedication to this principle is perhaps our most obvious characteristic and greatest asset in the struggle for existence, and we could not, if we would, find a completely desirable substitute for it. But we must recognize that it carries great liabilities when we are dealing with other people who may not have our dedication. Our Civil War was fought a century ago between two segments in our own society, one of which was considerably less dedicated to this principle than the other, and the lesson should be plain. The status quo cannot be preserved. Other peoples are having their civil wars today essentially on the same fundamental issue. Society and the individual everywhere must use and develop the discoveries and inventions of the human mind, and this means change, whether we, or other people, like it or not.

What the have-not peoples of the world want above all is a share in the science and technology that have made us powerful. Our democracy and our extravagant way of life, even if desirable, may seem a luxury which they can take or leave alone, but they know they cannot even protect the society they now have, much less achieve the society they may wish to have, without their share of the power that science and technology have brought to western civilization in general and to America in particular.

The distinguished British economist Barbara Ward has stated clearly what the impact of the American example has been: "Whether it is the political debate of equal rights to sovereign national independence and of equal political rights for citizens, or whether it is the economic drive of the 'Jeffersonian' idea—that political equality cannot be divorced from equal economic opportunity, the debate of 1776 is part of the world debate. The experiment of 1776 has set the terms of the argu-

ment, sharpened the issues and created the framework within
which all the great issues of world politics are now discussed.
The Thirteen Colonies, underdeveloped states some 180-odd
years ago, are now the leaders of a human column all of whom,
virtually without exception, march forward intent upon securing the same elbow room and sharing the same abundance. . . .
I would like to suggest to you," Miss Ward continues, "the possibility that, once a certain level of scientific, technological and industrial advance has been secured, one of the chief ways in
which we secure the materials we need for accomplishing our
purposes is simply by deciding to achieve them. . . . As the war
efforts of this century have shown, nations can vastly increase
their powers of production—America *doubled* its industrial
structure between 1940 and 1944—simply by setting themselves
more ambitious goals. And the reason is that the scientific
revolution has unleashed such capacity for expansion, such
powers of production, such ability to augment productivity that
imagination is now the chief limiting factor on what we can and
cannot produce. . . . People do what they want to do, make no
mistake about that." (*Spirit of '76—Why Not Now?* Williams-
burg, Va., 1963, p. 13-17 *passim*)

This is the heady example that the underdeveloped countries
of the world are taking, are insisting on taking, from the
American image today, as Miss Ward sees it. If a tiny nation like
Panama says to the United States occasionally, "Who do you
think you are, anyway?" we should be neither surprised nor un-
necessarily hurt that another child of the spirit of 1776 is reaching adolescence.

"People do what they want to," says Miss Ward, and her principal proof of this proposition is the American people. We may
argue that it just isn't so, but our most unguarded responses to
American society seem to me to suggest that Miss Ward has
stated our basic assumption. For example, when you meet someone for the first time and begin to get acquainted, after the *pro
forma* "How do you do?" the real question is "What do you do?"
In the course of the evening you may get around to "Who are
you?" (i.e., who are you kin to or a friend of, where from,
etc.)—but we are primarily interested in what people do, for to

an American this is the primary index to another American—
what he does and how well he does it—because we assume he is
doing what he wants to, and if he isn't he ought to be, or ought to
admit he's chicken!

There are times when we resent this assumption. We want to
be known and loved for ourselves, what we are rather than what
we do, but we don't have to go to the most widely used reference
book about Americans to be faced with the fact that *Who's Who*
is decided in terms of what we do. And perhaps even our friends
or lovers cannot know us for ourselves, what we are, save by
what we do.

It was scarcely necessary for me to tell this to the contingent
of the Peace Corps to whom I have referred. They represented as
well as any group I know the continuing evidence that mere images have not replaced ideals and that there is considerable inner-
direction evident in the American of today. Nor do I believe that
my contemporaries are any less committed than were their
ancestors to the principle that discoveries and inventions of the
human mind must change the status quo. But, if I could emphasize any one thing to those young people, I wanted it to be that
the traditional American meeting ground for ideals and reality
is in the pragmatic quest for solutions to human problems which
will not disappear of their own accord but which we must try to
solve, with practical measures, some hard sense, and not a little
charity, guided by our belief in the continuing viability of the
American proposition planted so ineradicably in our Declaration of Independence. That seed of social justice has not yet
grown to a mature plant even in the United States, and its ultimate fruit throughout the world is what other peoples are interested in.

One thing seems certain in human history. The society which
lacks a sustaining belief in its ideals cannot override another
society which possesses a sustaining belief. It is true that there
are other factors than belief which determine the ultimate outcome, over the years or the centuries, but no organism, physical
or social, can survive in the struggle for existence, even for the
purpose of eventual mutation, without sufficient spirit to sus-
tain the struggle. Perhaps the final lesson of the American Civil

War was not simply that a superior economy triumphed over an inferior economy but rather that, of two branches of American society, each believing strongly in its right, the one with both requirements for survival was able, at tremendous cost to itself, to subdue the other.

Just who do you think you are, anyway?

I remember with great affection a college professor who once wrote on a questionnaire, in the blank labeled "Character," concerning the student he was asked to recommend—"as to character, there is no doubt about his being one." That was, in my opinion, of more real value to the student's prospective employer, if the employer had enough sense to grasp its meaning, than all the character analysis a professor could have devoted to the subject.

From my observation, that is about the best that can be said about the American Character—the world can have no doubt about there being one. This was substantially what I said to the young men and women of the Peace Corps who later went to Africa to demonstrate the fact.

THE TASTE OF IT: OBSERVATIONS ON CURRENT EROTIC POETRY

At the conclusion of a recent poetry reading in the Coolidge
Auditorium of the Library of Congress, one elderly member of
the audience remarked to another, "What on earth has *happened*
to poetry?" The reply came, "The poet's privates are now public."

The question deserved a more comprehensive, and possibly a
more comprehending, response, although for succinctness
apropos, one could scarcely find fault with the description of
that portion of the reading to which the question and answer
were undoubtedly addressed. Since the reading was by one of
the poets discussed in the following pages, whose writing is by
no means extraordinary in the present milieu, perhaps an
historical perspective may not be amiss, in an effort to understand what seems to some an almost incredible happening.

At the turn of the century, Stephen Phillips let Marpessa's
lover admit, metaphorically, some interest in her body, but
climaxed his declaration with what was once a much admired
passage:

> Not for this only do I love thee, but
> Because Infinity upon thee broods;
> And thou art full of whispers and of shadows.

189

Thou meanest what the sea has striven to say
So long, and yearnèd up the cliffs to tell;
Thou art what all the winds have uttered not,
What the still night suggesteth to the heart.
(*Marpessa*, 1897)

With this romantic avowal of the mystical meaning in sexual
love, let us compare that of the lover speaking in the poem alluded
to in the first paragraph as the occasion for comment on its
public rendition by its author at the Library of Congress.

Going
from my known man's land
into the flowering country of woman.
Part of myself moving inside you gent-
ly or thrusting, kicking like an unborn child
in its development
Or like a live fish of silver or gold
now darting, now suspended quietly,
in your rich, profound, uncharted sea.
And you—you danced with me,
Sometimes led
        sometimes followed.

This is John Logan's "New Poem," *(Hudson Review,* Winter
1971-72, p. 631), thus far phrasing "the experience of sex" in
figures not unlike those of Stephen Phillips, though more intimate
certainly; but Logan continues less and less metaphorically—

as I felt you grip
    me and ungrip
        me
With your closing and opening body.

Thus far Stephen Phillips would scarcely have gone in his day.
But consider another of our contemporaries, Robert Creeley,
who has written ". . . . I felt her flesh/enclose mine. *Cock,*/they
say, *prick, dick,*/ I put it in her. I lay there." Perhaps poet John
Berryman may have had such a passage in mind when he wrote
of Creeley, "Sir, you are trivial." *(Love and Fame,* p. 24) But

when it comes to writing of love making, Berryman can be equally explicit: "you lay back on my thick couch in Manhattan/& opened yourself & said 'Kiss me.'/ I sucked your hairs." *(Ibid.,* p.52) That Berryman and Creeley practice widely divergent poetics makes their employment of sexual specifics even more to the point of this essay, as we shall see. Whether it is Paul Blackburn, like Creeley and other uninhibited poets of the Black Mountain school, describing "hot flesh/ socking it into hot flesh," *(The Cities,* "Park Poem," p.17) or Karl Shapiro, the *White Haired Lover,* dreaming of "rocketing into your loins/ And deep into your sea where no sun shines," (p.18) poetry has certainly come a long way since Stephen Phillips.

It would be difficult to drop back as far as Stephen Phillips' *Marpessa* to find a female poet so truly, if metaphorically, amorous in her language, but not many years apart there is Eunice Tietjens' "Psalm to My Beloved," beginning, "Lo, I have opened unto you the wide gates of my being,/ And like a tide you have flowed into me." *(A Book of Love Poems,* William Cole, ed., p.109) How old fashioned! Today we have Lenore Kandel in her "Love-Lust Poem," crying "I want to fuck you/I want to fuck you all the parts and places/I want you all of me/ . . . . your cock/ hard and strong/ grows stronger, throbs in my mouth/ . . . . your tongue slips wet and pointed and hot in my cunt/ . . . . you rise and lean over me/ and plunge that spit-slick cock into my depth. . . ."

Was this what Rimbaud had in mind when he prophesied that the forthcoming woman poet would discover "strange, unfathomable things, repulsive, delicious," and that "We shall take them, we shall understand them"? What imagery! What alliteration! And overall what a lay! This candle, guttering at both ends, may not last the night any better than Edna St. Vincent Millay's did, but there can be little doubt that it gives a raunchier light. If you doubt, look for the entire poem, which quite probably may remain the *ne plus ultra* paean to physiological techniques of erotic ecstasy. Who was it said "anything a man can do, a woman can do better"?

But what about homosexual lovers? Remember the lament of Stephen Phillips' contemporary, Oscar Wilde, who wished "To

drift with every passion till my soul / Is a stringed lute on which
all winds can play, /. . . . lo! with a little rod / I did but touch
the honey of romance — / And must I lose a soul's inheritance?"
(Modern British Poetry, ed. Louis Untermeyer, p. 67).

The pathos of Wilde's lament cannot be escaped, but for the
genuinely shattering poetry of buggery, we must come to Allen
Ginsberg: "That's that / yes yes / the flat cocks the red pricks
the gentle pubic hair / along with me / my magic spell. My
power /what I desire alone / what after thirty years /I got
forever / after thirty years / satisfied enough with Peter / with
all I wanted / with many men I knew one generation / our sperm
passing / into our mouths and bellies / beautiful when love /
given." *(Airplane Dreams, Composition from a Journal,* p. 7)
Ginsberg's paeans to "the heat of desire/ like shit in my
asshole," *(Ibid.,* p. 6) do not, however, soar always thus on cloud
69, for homosexual love has its own pathos, plumbed with the
memorable line, "and who wants to get fucked up the ass,
really?" *(Kaddish,* p.84)

There is perhaps no more obvious example of the impact of
contrasting social environments on the literary artist, than the
contrast between Wilde's essentially ambivalent sexuality and
sophisticated art on the one hand, and Ginsberg's terribly
dedicated homosexuality and "sincere" verse on the other.
Wilde's brilliant but frequently superficial wit and decadent use
of metaphor, not to relate but to obfuscate, with both a sigh and
a giggle, was as certainly a product of his *fin de siècle,* art-for-
art's-sake, but nevertheless bourgeois-British milieu, as is Ginsberg's naked, animal bellowing and sincere avowal of his "or"
rather than "either or" sexuality, a product of our own era of
live-in-your-guts reality, yet never-the-less also bourgeois
milieu, derived from Emerson and Whitman, and further taught
by a century of "scientific" truth. But let us not get ahead of schedule in analyzing the taste of our age.

Between Wilde and Ginsberg, we must not forget the supreme
spectacle of metaphorical buggery at its peak of British literary
insouciance, brought up on Freud and Marx, but scoffing as
often as not at both. Certainly the veritable D'Artagnan of those
famous musketeers of Platonic Oxford was W. H. Auden, whose

incomparable rhythms in such poems as "Heavy Date," are buggery's best:

> When I was a child, I
> Loved a pumping-engine,
> Thought it every bit as Beautiful as you. (*Collected Shorter Poems*, p. 153)

But let no one forget that his lines to homosexual love number some of the finest lyrics of any kind written in English: "Lay your sleeping head, my love,/ Human on my faithless arm." (*Ibid.*, 107) Yet, Auden, like Wilde, put his homosexuality into metaphor rather than physiological specifics.

At this point can we discard once and for all the suspicion that what we have before us can be dismissed as pornography, obscene and "hard core," whatever that may mean, either *in* or *out* of "context," whatever that may mean? All these are poets, genuine enough, though our purpose here is not to rank any of them, and they write of a human experience, each in his own way in his own time, which is our time, not Chaucer's or Sappho's. Auden's "Ode to the Medieval Poets" asks how *they* ever managed "without anesthetics or plumbing" to "write so cheerfully,/ with no grimace of self-pathos?" (*Poetry*, Chicago, November 1971) And does one wonder how, without benefit of Freud or Kinsey, Sappho could? There may be a hint in her famous verses to Oneirus, god of dreams:

> . . . O soothing god
> Who warns me of the tension and the strife
> of keeping burning wish and act apart:
> I do not think that I shall spurn the truth of
> what you've shown,
> for, with the Blessed One's support,
> I shall by no means not
> grasp the thing for which I groan.
> (Paul Roche, *Love Songs of Sappho*, p. 32)

Such a naive pagan, "suckled in a creed outworn" perhaps, has certain advantages that not even a Lenore Kandel can muster today, for modern poets seem unable to escape poetic "self-

consciousness," whether, as in Auden's "Ode," they are "morose
or/ kinky, petrified by their gorgon egos. " Far from being eman-
cipated from the tyranny of sex, the modern poet has problems
that one suspects the ancients never dreamed of at worst. A
modern Sappho, Elizabeth Sargent, who prints as epigraph to
her *Love Poems* the passage from Rimbaud previously cited,
sets forth beautifully the ethical, psychological, and physical
hangups of the modern poet. Sappho and her male or female contemporaries might, quite simply and sincerely, pray for a good
tumescence and a good orgasm, where your modern may only
wish, but here is Elizabeth Sargent's confession:

WE POETS*
We poets always think our poems will bring love.
You hate the electric years charged in my raw
Nerves; I have loved and made love, but not like this
We poets always think our poems will bring love.
You say I know too many men, that I make coarse
Scenes: I frighten you with my desperate kiss
We poets always hope our poems may bring love,
Everything we want is against the law
We crave mind and body and soul (the light) so
        we aim for a weak place and we don't miss
Forgive us our curious love
Forgive our shameful turbulence—Yes!
Rub the place of shame, rub it hard
With your hard flesh   We poets wish our poems
                                 would bring love
Yes! (O yes) We have loved and made love before
But not like this.
                    (*Love Poems*, New American Library, p. 16)

What we have been gleaning, need it be emphasized, is not
atypical; it is perhaps only a bit more memorable in poetic concentration than what one expects, and finds, in fiction, drama,
and even especially of late, in movies, or, of course, in those
medical, psychiatric, or whatever "scientific" studies, with
which we have been deluged since Freud. In the alphabetical

* Quoted by permission of Elizabeth Sargent.

sequence, at least from Barth and Burroughs through Updike and Vidal, American prose authors are likewise all at it.

And it is merely one, though a dominant, aspect of a large question— what has happened?

We have been considering the poet's treatment of sexual love because it presents the clearest, or most obvious, evidence of the shift in point-of-view, frame-of-reference. or "attitude" to human life as merely one aspect of the whole of nature, a shift which has taken place almost entirely in the twentieth century, and all too slowly according to ecologists. The tradition which shapes the individual literary talent in such recent poetry clearly derives not so much from the humanism of Cardinal Newman and Matthew Arnold via T. S. Eliot, much less via Irving Babbitt or Paul Elmer More, as from the naturalism of Charles Darwin and Thomas H. Huxley via Sigmund Freud and Alfred Kinsey. This frame of reference is that of the evolutionary life-tree in the background, linking man's basic kinship with the animals on every limb. As today's poet sees himself, he is a repository and recapitulation of that life, the rudiments of which are an alimentary system with orifices for ingesting and excreting, the textures of which, lips and anus, are so nearly alike that scientific description employs almost identical terminology for them, except to differentiate their respective basic functions. Indeed, whereas the psalmist conceived himself as "a little lower than the angels," the modern poet recognizes himself as only somewhat above the worm, but with the same oral and anal pleasures, presumably, as identified by Freud. The enormity of complexities clustered around, and en route between, those extremities is, again presumably, man's alone, and provides the context of twentieth century "humanism" from *The Magic Mountain* to the depths of *The Valley of the Dolls.* To the complaint that this is a dehumanizing frame-of-reference and does not deserve the name of humanism, one can reply that it is at least no less centered on human interests and values, however much those have changed, as presented by zoologist Desmond Morris' scientific popularizations, *The Naked Ape* and *Intimate Behavior.*

Remembering Hamlet's apostrophe to man, we might rephrase his words somewhat thus: What a piece of work is

man! in action how like an ape! in apprehension how like a
worm! the paradigm of animals! And yet to me what is this
quintessence of slime? Man enthalls me! Yes, and woman too!
   But one need not rephrase Charles Olson's succinct apostrophe
to man: "A zoo/ is what he's come to, the old/ Beginner, the old/
Winner/ Who took all,/ for awhile." (*Selected Writings*, p. 189)
Poets who cling to a traditional religious point of view may, of
course, still believe with Brother Antoninus (William Everson)
that "Though lying with woman,/ Taking deep joy from her rich
knees,/ Or threshing that dream in the lonely circle of masturbation,/or seeking it locked in a boy's limbs,/. . . . Be sure your
joy breeds from a beauty/ Existent beyond it and out of its
reach. . . ." (*The Residual Years*, p. 104) This essentially Christian point of view is not greatly different, however, from the
neo-Brahamanism of Lenore Kandel's "Invocation for Maitreya,"
with "the warm moist fabric of the body opening into star-shot
rose flowers/ the dewy cock effulgent as it bursts the star/
sweet cunt-mouth of the world serpent Ouroboros girding the uni-
verse/ as it takes its own eternal cock, and cock and cunt united
join the circle/ moving through realms of flesh made fantasy
and fantasy made flesh. . . ." (*Word Alchemy*, p. 13) And indeed, Brother Antoninus' *The Rose of Solitude* seems to cast just
this mystical point of view into acceptable (to him) Christian
poetics.
   Whatever mystical possibilities there may be for the mystic,
the modern poet, male or female, usually addresses sexuality
primarily for itself, although this is not to say that there is not
much romantic tenderness in it. For example, Anne Sexton's
description of "the music for which I was born": "Lock in! Be
alert my acrobat/ and I will be soft wood and you the nail/ and
we will make fiery ovens for Jack Sprat/ and you will hurl
yourself into my tiny jail/ and we will take a supper together
and that/ will be that." (*Love Poems*, p. 67) Or consider the conclusion of Robert Watson's tender "Do you Love Me?": "Such odd
handles, pouches, spouts, and pipes/ That twitch, swell, or
spurt. Like dish washing,/ Done, then time to start again.
Dignity?/ Animals have it over man." (*Christmas in Las Vegas*,
p. 47) In spite of tenderness, one detects in both these poets a
sense that sexual love seems pointless and empty, a crassly
repetitive waste,— "That will be that" or "Done, then time to

start again." Far from being momentous, sex has become merely momentary.

This attitude, which seems to permeate so much modern literature, presents many a variation on Freud's idea that life exists for death, with its corollary that expenditure of sexual energy (eros) is merely the wasting toward extinction, which civilized man through art and religion to some extent sublimates into the more meaningful (at least one hopes so) symbolic detritus of dream, myth, or poem. Biological progeny, Darwin to the contrary, seems to provide poets such inadequate, not to say downright disappointing results! Perhaps this recognition of the essentially wasteful nature of the sexual act is today the ultimate significance of all art, as well as life, and may provide the final clue to what is happening to poetry, if one seeks far enough.

The modern poet pursues to the source the physiological implications of sex and concentrates on the neural endings whence its sensation arises. So ecstasy is defined, if not devaluated, as orgasm, and orgasm is neurally fixed where, as Yeats wrote, "Love has pitched his mansion in/ the place of excrement." ("Crazy Jane Talks with the Bishop," *Collected Poems*, p. 255) There it becomes no mansion, however, for those who insist on ruling their own roost: *vide* Norman Mailer, *The Prisoner of Sex*, almost a poem!

The title of Marshall McLuhan's paper-back gospel, with what one at first assumed to be a typographical error, is not inappropriate for a great mass of recent literature, *The Medium is the Massage [sic]*, but for our increasingly explicit and physical poets it would be exquisitely accurate to name, in Ginsberg's phrase, "the come of the poem." (*Reality Sandwiches*, p. 51) Commonly, little metaphor, mystery, or meaning beyond the denotation sets off poetic description from the scientific language of the sexual laboratory specialists William H. Masters and Virginia E. Johnston (*Human Sexual Response*), though all poets seem to prefer a higher charge of sensuousness and a higher percentage of Anglo-Saxon mixed with their Latin plainspeak, and some still employ the mystique of symbol and metaphor. The frame-of-reference is, however, the same. Of course, poets as well as novelists write of other matters than sex, but sex is the center of the vortex from which they view what Charles

Olson has named "the human universe." In the words of James Dickey's Appalachian woman preacher, "the county speaks of nothing/ Else each year at this time: speaks as beasts speak to themselves/ Of holiness learned in the barn." ("May Day Sermon," *Poems 1957-1967*, p. 12)

Somewhat to offset the negative impact of the scientific view, there has developed the notion that science, by destroying faith and belief in deity, has merely prepared humanity for a return to mythic patterns of early, pre-Christian civilization, and that by questing in T. S. Eliot or James Joyce, with the aid of apostles like Joseph Campbell (*The Masks of God* and *Hero with a Thousand Faces*) and assorted professors of literature, one finds guidance. But this is just a notion, as often scorned as it is accepted by poets today. However valuable the theories, likewise, of Freud and Jung, they are not gospel to a poet like the cunning John Berryman, for example. Moderns tend to be typically agnostic about theory and creed alike. And indeed, it would seem that like older myths, Christian orthodoxy, either Roman or Protestant, supplies but temporary refuge even to an Allen Tate or a Robert Lowell, and to an Auden it would seem to be merely a modern version of the medieval mountebank's faith in the juggler's art. Thus the modern poet who has lost a religion seems to be becoming not a mythologist so much as a neo-pythagorean, who sees himself in the life cycle at one with the worm near the other end of the evolutionary schema, and frequently more confused by his extremities. As Berryman has put it so aptly, "Everybody's mouth/ is somewhere else, I know, somebody's anus." (*His Toy, His Dream, His Rest*, p. 104) And although Lenore Kandel's vision of "world serpent" taking its "own eternal cock" in its own "cunt-mouth" may be at least possible for the earth worm as well as the serpent, it presents insoluble problems of logistics for humans, though an approximate solution is reached by J. V. Cunningham's "Lip":

Lip was a man who used his head
He used it when he went to bed
With his friend's wife, and with his friend,
With either sex at either end. (*Collected Poems*, p. 118)

When Cunningham read this poem in the Coolidge Auditorium of the Library of Congress, it may be remarked, the audience seemed too startled for comment; or, perhaps, recognizing the implicit puritanism of the poet's satire, simply made allowance because of his avowed eschewal of four letter words. He said simply: "Most of my contempories don't know how to be dirty. The first inviolable rule is: never use a dirty word." (*National Poetry Festival, Proceedings*, Washington, 1964, p. 197)

The attractiveness of some variety of worm for poetic contemplation, particularly with regard to sex, crops up repeatedly in modern verse. Thus Karl Shapiro, "As a slug on the flat of the sun-heated clay,/ With the spit of its track left behind it like glass./. . . So my tongue on the white-heated wall of your thigh/. . . And the slug of our wetness finds green food among/ The hair-forests of longing where serpents uncoil." (*The Place of Love*, p. 64) But perhaps it has been the Australian poet A.D. Hope who has most sardonically hoisted "for our age a symbol," in his poem "The Kings," extolling "the great greedy parasitic worm":

> Alone among the royal beasts of prey
> He takes no partner, no imperial mate
> Seeks his embrace and bears his clamorous brood;
> Within himself, in soft and passionate play,
> Two sexes in their vigor celebrate
> The raptures of helminthine solitude, (*Collected Poems*, p. 99)

Of course, Hope's metaphorical method is not new, anymore than his Byronic prosody. More than a century ago, the witty doctor Oliver Wendell Holmes reached far down in the zoological kingdom for his symbolic "Chambered Nautilus," perhaps with tongue in scientific cheek, to illustrate the taste of his age for the pious moral and the pretty object. But no modern poet in whatever insistently modern verse has phrased a satirical modern view better than Hope. This triumph of zoology has been a large price to pay, but Hope demonstrates in several poems that art can play vizier to *that* sultan, and use him for other than his own ends. Not every modern poet comes off so well with scientific realism. Certainly no modern poet could possibly fancy, as Wordsworth did, his new-born infant "trailing clouds of glory," but Galway Kinnell risks a great deal in "this peck/ of stunned flesh/ clotted with celestial cheesiness." ("Under the Maud Moon," *The Book of Nightmares,* p. 6) Let's call this, at most, a draw. And Sylvia Plath risks (but wins?) even more in "The baby smiles, fat snail." ("Lesbos," *Ariel,* p. 30) A biological orientation is not always pleasant for the poet to live with.

In the last quarter century, a good deal of poetic push has been against the nineteenth century romantic (i.e., Emersonian) conception of reality (Nature) as symbol of divine non-reality. The poet now sees and names the reality, and *this* is poetry. Hence metaphor in the traditional sense, as the essence of poetry, for Frost no less than Shakespeare, is scorned, and the figure of speech is either denounced or ridiculed. So Charles Olson, defending William Carlos Williams' proposition "Not in ideas but in things," deposes: "If there is any clue to what an image is today, Linnaeus—or Agassiz, for that matter—are better informants than all writers other than the handful of Americans who have been on the job recently. . . ." ("Projective Verse," *The Human Universe and Other Essays,* p. 60) Presumably the poets he means are the Black Mountaineers, Olson, Creeley, Blackburn, Jonathan Williams, et al. But one does not always so easily, either by erudite or illiterate insistence, escape the trap of language. Even in their insistence on common English for sexual love,—e.g., Creeley's "say *prick, dick*"— they are sometimes less the poet than is Susan Norris in her "Nothing for the Ladies": "Well, honey, I finally figured out I got a/ vagina, but now dat ain't so bad. A vagina a/ penis inside out/ . . . .It proverb time honey/ an orgasm in de vagina worth two in the hand/ What dat sound like/ a bird in de hand, worth 2 bird in de bush/ (come on you guys, is masturbating really that much/ better than screwing/. . . , I am a woman/ I am nothing/ I do nothing/ but nothing is/ something/ inside out." (*Evergreen Review,* August 1968) *There* is a poet who knows, whether she has looked it up or not, the mere metaphor and the ambiguity of Creeley's *"prick,"* when the first meaning in *Webster's Colle-*

giate is the hole and the second the instrument that makes the hole. And what teenager today does not know the meaning of the verb "make"? Thus Thomas Gray's tritest truth, "Where ignorance is bliss. . . ."

Olson goes whole hog, of course, in discipleship to William Carlos Williams, by setting up for himself and his own followers an entirely zoological approach to prosody. His theory of "projective verse" insists that "breath is man's special qualification as animal. Sound is a dimension he has extended. Language is one of his proudest acts. And when a poet rests in those as they are in himself (in his physiology, if you like, but the life in him for all of that) then he, if he chooses to speak from these roots, works in that area where nature has given him size, projective size." (*Human Universe*, p. 60) John Logan has particularized Olson's anatomical abstractions, speaking to a University of Maryland Symposium. ". . .as a loner reaching out to you with the long penis of my tongue of poems, showering the sperm of my syllables and breathing on you with the passion of my warm breath. . ." ("Poets and Poetry Today," *Voyages*, IV, III and IV, Issues — 12/13, p. 24)

To conclude examination of our frame-of-reference, this survey has been obviously selective, but one believes significant. The psalmist's question "What is man?" remains in need of an answer satisfactory, or at least meaningful, to the agonizing present. In Michael McClure's notorious play *The Beard*, Billy the Kid says to Jean Harlow, "You wouldn't know divine from a handful of shit. . . ." She replies, "If you're divine I'd rather be elsewhere!" And the dialogue continues:

The Kid: Lying on a bed with a magazine?

Harlow: Yeah.

The Kid: You'd be divine there too.

Harlow: You said I wouldn't know divine from a handful of shit!

The Kid: You wouldn't know it but you'd be there!

To such an epiphany for existentialists, perhaps Allen Ginsberg has provided the consummate line: "The whole universe a shaggy dog story." ("Laughing Gas," *Kaddish,* p. 69)

Thus we come to the question of esthetics. To begin, we may restate our point-of-view, or attitude. Much significant thinking about esthetics today has a scientific, or more specifically an anthropological, frame-of-reference. Whether one studies music, dance, sculpture, painting, or literature, he can escape the futility of repetitious old fogeyism best by knowing where the action is. What Thomas Aquinas thought about "beauty," as Joyce's Stephen discovered *(Portrait of the Artist as a Young Man),* makes sense today, if at all, only in the scholastic frame-of-reference in which Aquinas lived and thought his monkish life out. In principle, the same can be said about Freud's commentary on *Hamlet,* or Coleridge's commentary on the same subject, for that matter. And when Wilfrid Mellers writes on "Pop as Ritual in Modern Culture" (*Times Literary Supplement,* November 19, 1971), he tells us something about both "pop" and modern culture which seems to some to make more sense than what every music critic knows. That he also illustrates, in another form of expression, the theme we are pursuing here is not beside the point either.

Yet, even the poets we have been discussing tend to be traditional and moralistic when they turn literary critics, and begin flogging each other from opposing camps. Karl Shapiro speaks to the subject thus: "The down hill speed of American poetry in the last decade has been breathtaking for those who watch the sport. Poetry plunged out of the classics, out of the modern masters, out of all standards, and plopped into the playpen. There we are entertained with the fecal-buccal carnival of the Naughties and the Uglies, who have their own magazines and publishing houses, and the love-lorn alienates, nihilists, disaffiliates who croon or 'rock' their way into the legitimate publishing establishment." ("The Poetry Wreck," *Library Journal,* February 15, 1970, p. 634) This debacle, Shapiro claims, "began with *Howl,* a high-falutin put-on which started up the seismographs of Berkeley and elsewhere." Shapiro's qualifications for so critically speaking, he believes, are demonstrated by his own work and by his discipleship to Henry Miller and D. H. Lawrence, as well as his long defense of "absolute unqualified freedom to print and present anything and everything the human mind and sub-mind are capable of advancing."

When the author of *Howl* speaks, however, to the same general subject, he finds that the true geniuses are the likes of Michael McClure, Gary Snyder, and Gregory Corso. The last named, he dubs "Genius, absolutely, irrevocably, line by line, invented phrase by invented phrase, death thrill by politic prophecy. . ." etc., etc., (*The New York Times Book Review*, April 4, 1971). We may illustrate by a few lines, neither best nor worst, but merely Corso: "Behind the wheel Death, a big sloppy faggot; / He opened the door I *had* to get in! / For one whole year he sucked me off, and I always came!" ("Greece," *Long Live Man*, p. 26) When Ginsberg speaks of the "thousands and thousands of active heads" for whom "Corso or Snyder have actually defined large areas of our communal Consciousness," he is not referring to the listening millions who think poetry is nothing but the accompaniment for guitar music, whom Shapiro seems to believe to be one common audience, although there is probably as much overlapping of those two audiences as there is of the audiences of *Sewanee Review* and *Atlantic Monthly*, respectively. He means the thousands who *buy* and read the paperback poetry of Corso, Snyder, or Ginsberg, as published to taste.

One might try to mediate the conflicting judgments of Shapiro and Ginsberg with the kind of thinking George Orwell employs in his essay on *Gulliver's Travels*. "Part of our minds — in any normal person it is the dominant part — believes that man is a noble animal and life is worth living; but there is also a sort of inner self which at least intermittently stands aghast at the horror of existence. In the queerest way, pleasure and disgust are linked together. The human body is beautiful; it is also repulsive and ridiculous. . . ." True, but useless as an esthetic for defining or describing poetry, or any other art. All Orwell does is state the ambivalence of human nature toward art, which is the same ambivalence that human nature holds toward life, as Swift exemplifies, and Shapiro, and Ginsberg.

There was once a distinguished though neglected critic who thought he had a solution to our problem. Sadly, the title of his once famous essay, "The New Criticism," became appropriated by a school of critics whose disciples ruled the academic establishment so effectively as to all but obliterate his memory by simple neglect, although some of them embarked from the same pier of the critical domain; namely, that the critic should ask what the creator aimed to do and whether he hit the mark. Joel Elias Spingarn undertook to jettison all of "scholarly" and "literary" criticism, following Croce, "who has led aesthetic thought inevitably from the concept that art is expression to the conclusion that all expression is art." Spingarn's logic culminated in the proposition that "taste must reproduce the work of art within itself in order to understand and judge it; and at that moment aesthetic judgment becomes nothing more nor less than creative art itself." (*Creative Criticism*, 1917) His valedictory sentence ends with the claim that "the art of criticism . . . serves as some sort of mirror to the art of literature, only because in their flashes of insight taste and genius are one."

At this point, one would only suggest that Spingarn in 1917 was more of a prophet than a literary critic, for he described then more accurately than anyone has since what seems to be the esthetic of the age we now seem to have entered.

The poet Ned O'Gorman, in an article entitled "The Electric Nunc," largely agreeing with Karl Shapiro concerning recent poetry, makes a casual remark that tells more than perhaps his satiric jest intended. "It is no longer possible to walk into the Museum of Modern Art and not be careful about bumping into the most innocuous pile of cigarette butts, dust, and matchsticks for fear it may be a 'work of art.' Just so, one must be watchful of a desperately major part of the new work that is pure rotten poetry. Masked as 'art,' it just is not." (*Cultural Affairs*, Fall 1970) How sure can this poet-critic be? Is it possible that ecology is providing the frame-of-reference for the modern esthetic, just as zoology is doing for love poetry?

If Claes Oldenburg is a genius at depicting cigarette butts, it may be because he intuitively sees in the world around him the significance that "reason" is just now (and with what reluctance!) beginning to discover about the age of science and technology. Then what about the museum janitor who leaves a pile of dust, butts, and matchsticks conspicuously on the museum floor? Is life imitating art, consciously or subconsciously? Or, perhaps a janitor has his own personal esthetic and expresses it for those campy, litter-bug art lovers who stroll in the Museum of Modern Art!

Admitting both the vision and the technique of the junkyard school of sculpture to be peculiarly relevant today, does one have to "appreciate" the enshrinement of junk only on a pedestal? Obviously a beer can in the gutter as well as the dog turd on the curb (one always hopes it was a dog) is an "esthetic expression," in the root meaning of the words, no less than an image of them on a modern artist's canvas, or in the poem of a modern poet.

Of course, we must not equate the modern poet or sculptor with the patient in a mental institution who habitually deposits his bowel movement in the middle of his cell floor, and then waits, contemplating it philosophically in perhaps Tantric (for all you or I know) complexities of esthetic meaning, until an attendant comes to clean it up. But they do have something in common, it would seem, in their preoccupation with waste, the common denominator of civilization, as well as nature. The fires of nature are alternately stoked and smothered by waste, and civilization battens and chokes on waste, celebrates it (the death of heroes!), and, in so far as can be, is preserved by it and ultimately covered by its detritus.

It is literally as well as symbolically true (Is there a difference?) that what we know of man, as far back as we can go historically and archaeologically, is his detritus—used remnants and waste. And likewise, of an individual now or then, who happens to be a poet, what we know are the used remnants and waste of his creative being, to which he has given some sort of poetic form. This waste endures its span, short or long, as the hint or implication of being, and this we call art, as we learn to know it by perceiving it. The quality of the perception has been called by the name "taste," and this alone distinguishes both the making and the recognition of art from the discovery and recognition of truth.

Perhaps the exemplar par excellence of this modern esthetic is the poet Merrill Moore, who tapped his streaming consciousness for an average of five sonnets per day over a period of thirty years. Moore looms as a protean modern genius, using his poems as he used paper towels, wiping with and discarding rather than embroidering and laundering, "filling and emptying waste baskets," actually and symbolically, day by day, and nonchalantly asking the sixty-four-dollar question:

> Who considers the contents of waste baskets
> Of negligible or supernumerary worth? ("The Contents of Waste
> Baskets," *M,* p. 324)

So the poet, the dog, the sculptor, and the insane male confined from the date of his military disability for "breakdown" in combat—all "make" something symbolic of the age in which they live, and each of us may meditate and/or appreciate its significance, as Allen Ginsberg spells it right out of the *Oxford English Dictionary* in its most elemental form.

So beautiful!—as doting mamma Portnoy might exclaim—then why do you need a poetry, please? An answer by one of the masters of modern esthetics, James Joyce, was put in the mouth of Malachi Mulligan concerning the contemplation of a wine bottle: "Any object, intensely regarded, may be a gate of access to the incorruptible eon of the gods." (*Ulysses,* Penguin Edition, p. 413). This is the nub of the modern esthetic. Contemplate and write it down, bottle, can, pile of trash, or just plain crap! Thus the junk yard of rusting Fords and Chevrolets is an epiphany, whether or not assisted by the blow-torch-and-metal-shears sculptor into the pure (abstract or concrete?) art on the pedestal. Even the heavens no longer merely, in the words of the psalmist, "declare the glory of God," as they once did. Abandoned rocket hulls join the stars in the firmament! And only the Spiro Agnews can fail to see that it is not only the poets, artists, and professors who have instructed the young. The establishment itself has expressed the largest pile of all, which no doubt calls for a functional poet, in words of praise, to ritualize into an appropriate epiphany for all of us. Would Mr. O'Gorman like to lead us in *that* prayer?

Having written thus, one is not surprised to be told by a spoil-sport first reader that these ideas are not precisely new, since Georges Bataille, whom one has never read, spent many years evolving his comprehensive philosophy of waste. Of course, the ancients were not unaware of what was happening in their day either, as *Ecclesiastes* and *Mahabharata* testify, no less than Wallace Stevens in a modern view of

> . . . the immense detritus of a world
> That is completely waste, that moves from waste
> To waste, out of the hopeless waste of the past
> Into a hopeful waste to come.
> ("The Statue at the World's End," *The Man with the Blue Guitar and Other Poems*, 1937, p. 47)

And indeed the avant reader may judge my theme as well as my illustrations to be somewhat banal, a verdict which will indicate both his and my point of view. The taste of it is in the mouth. Scientific rationalism, from Darwin via Freud and Kinsey, posited early in this essay to have been apparently more in-fluential than the humanism of Newman via Eliot, may be merely an appearance, misleading for what lies underneath. The vista of Eliot's asymbolic Waste Land seems already turning into well-manured reality landscape, seen through eyes gifted with understanding *The Greening of America*. Who can tell?

Yet, maybe poetry will serve, if one possesses sufficient zest. William Carlos Williams exulted: "I'll put this in my diary:/ On my 65th birthday/ I kissed her while she pissed." (*Collected Later Poems*, p. 204) And Allen Ginsberg phrased the ambiguity of esthetic cause and effect: It's hard to eat shit, without having visions." (*Reality Sandwiches*, p. 47) But a contemporary of Stephen Phillips, A. E. Housman, who also knew the human condition from personal experience as well as from poetry, pointed the moral of his "Epilogue" perhaps more to the taste of some, with the fable of the king who got used to eating poison every day: "Mithradates, he died old."